D1453963

RORY MOULTON

# Essential Rome Travel Tips

*Secrets, Advice & Insight for Planning the Perfect Rome Vacation*

EE EuroExperto

# Contents

III   Indulge

# Preface

Rome is Western civilization's cultural heartbeat. Its ancient ruins, juxtaposed against modern Metro stations, vintage Vespas and vibrant street murals, capture the imagination. Its cuisine draws foodies from around the world. Its state within a state, Vatican City, beckons Christians and non-Christians alike to come pay homage. Rome is like nowhere else on Earth.

Since you've bought this book, you're planning on or at least considering a trip to Rome. Let me state emphatically: You're making a life-altering choice. Even after you depart, Rome will linger in your dreams, tugging at you to return. You'll never forget her Mediterranean sunsets, the way that first taste of Frascati wine felt against your tongue and how that first glance of the Colosseum sent goosebumps up and down your arms. Rome is eternal.

## How to Use this Guide

In this little book, I've collected and boiled down all the best travel tips and recommendations I've gathered over 20 years of visiting Rome. Some tips I learned the hard way. Others were handed down to me from veteran "Romers." (No one actually calls them that.) Still more I figured out with my family, my always-willing guinea pigs.

The book is divided into three sections:

1. Survive & Thrive: Practical information for planning your trip and navigating this tangled city.
2. Go » See » Do: Sightseeing tips and tricks for avoiding crowds at the city's top sights and advice for exploring away from the crowds.
3. Indulge: How to eat and drink your way around Rome like a savvy local.

In each chapter, I include links to Google Maps and helpful websites. I strongly recommend you download and learn to use Google Maps and the apps in the "Five Killer Apps" chapter. I find the more learning and organizing I do on my phone before a trip, the less I fiddle around with it during my trip. And that's a good thing.

Website URLs are left in their original length unless they're ridiculously long. In which case, I've shortened them using a service called bit.ly. Don't worry—they're safe to click.

Speaking of websites, Italy's state-run websites are notoriously unreliable. Sites go down for long periods of maintenance with no word on when or if they'll return. What I'm trying to say is, the links in this book might not always work.

Prices change. So do operating hours. Always check ahead. In fact, I've intentionally omitted pricing for most attractions and activities. Click the website link for updated pricing (fingers crossed the website works...). I do list operating hours, but, again, they change all the time.

Finally, I include this in every book I write: This is just a guide, an outline. Use it to devise your trip of a lifetime to Rome. Ignore or follow my advice as you see fit. And buy a couple other guidebooks (that's something you don't often hear from my fellow travel writers). I typically purchase 3-4 books per trip.

It's a small investment relative to your total trip budget.

So, there you have it. The Eternal City is now at your fingertips. I'm so excited for you. Maybe we'll meet for a gelato in a floodlit piazza some day. I'd like that. Until then, however, *ciao!*

# FREE Paris eBook

Receive a FREE Paris ebook today.

After downloading your free book, you'll receive a monthly VIP email with book giveaways, new book announcements and huge book discounts ONLY available exclusively to subscribers.

Join the crew and subscribe for **FREE** to Rory Moulton's monthly email newsletter about European travel, "*EuroExperto*." In addition to the giveaways and discounts, receive the month's best European travel articles, news, tips, trends and more. I'll never spam you. I don't do ads. And you can unsubscribe at any time.

Smarter European travel is just a click away:

rorymoulton.com/subscribe

# FREE Travel Planning Email Courses

These 100% free email courses break down daily itineraries into digestible and customizable travel plans. Sent every morning on consecutive days, my travel-planning email courses will help you put together a trip that maximizes your time and budget, while minimizing itinerary potholes. Sign up today and your course begins tomorrow.

## 10 Perfect Days in Paris

Over five daily emails, we'll map out exactly where to go, how to get there and even provide suggestions for restaurants and picnic locations along the way. With over 5,000 graduates, this is our most-popular email course to date.

**Sign up:** bit.ly/perfectpariscourse

## 3 Blissful Days in Amsterdam

Three high-intensity sightseeing days scour Amsterdam's biggest sights, coolest neighborhoods, tastiest foodie haunts and feistiest night spots. You'll receive three daily emails breaking down exactly what to see and do and where to shop, eat and drink.

**Sign up:** bit.ly/3daysamsterdam

# Also by Rory Moulton

## Essential Paris Travel Tips

*"A very worthwhile tool when planning a Paris visit. Author presents idea after idea and ways to save anyone time and money... Worth every penny for this easy to use guide."*
5/5 stars, Amazon Best Seller
**Buy Now:** amzn.to/2yVdKV1

## Essential Amsterdam Travel Tips

*"Highly recommended with plenty of useful information. Light reading unlike other travel books – website links embedded are very helpful. Well worth the price."*
5/5 Stars, Amazon Best Seller
**Buy Now:** amzn.to/2Qjp3Nn

## Hiking France

Hike through pastoral countryside, stopping in beautiful villages, tasting wine at storied vineyards, sleeping in historic hotels, shopping country markets, stumbling upon Roman ruins and eating in some of Europe's best restaurants. **Coming in 2021!**

# I

# Survive & Thrive

*Practicalities – Orientation – Transportation – Safety*

# 1

# Ciao! (Survival Italian)

U nless you already speak Italian, no one expects you to learn the language in a matter of months. As great as Rosetta Stone and Babbel are, they'll only get you so far. Yet, I strongly recommend learning basic phrases, pleasantries and greetings. "Survival Italian," as I like to call it. Using what little Italian you know will go a long way in separating you from the tourist pack. Try your Italian and watch the locals smile with pride.

But this advice comes with a caveat: As much as Italians love to hear tourists attempting to speak their language, this is a hustle-and-bustle city. Shop clerks, waiters, bartenders are not your free language tutors. Lead with the Italian you have, but don't expect help. And don't bother asking for language tips. You'll likely receive an answer in accented, but perfectly serviceable English.

Don't worry, though. You will nail some indispensable phrases. And you will use them as you stride confidently through Rome's open markets, boutique shops and piazza cafes. And just to reassure you, most Romans will speak English with you, often enthusiastically.

So, there's no need to study for the Italian AP exam. But keep in mind three rules as you navigate basic Italian:

1. Italian is phonetic. It's spoken exactly as it's written.
2. Pronunciation rules are constant.
3. Every letter is pronounced. There are no silent letters.

Remember those three rules, master the following phrases and you'll quickly separate yourself from Rome's tourist morass:

- Yes/No :: **Sì/No** :: *See/No*
- Hello/Goodbye :: **Ciao** :: *chow*
- Please :: **Per favore** :: *pair fav-aw-ray*
- Thank you :: **Grazie** :: *graz-ee-ay*
- You're welcome :: **Prego** :: *pray-go*
- Excuse me :: **Scusami** :: *scoo-sa-mee.*
- Speak English? :: **Parla inglese?** :: *par-la een-glay-say?*
- The check please :: **Il conto per favore** :: *eel kon-tow pair fav-aw-ray*
- Where is the toilet? :: **Dov'è il bagno?** :: *doh-veh eel bah-nyoh?*
- How much does it cost? :: **Quanto costa?** :: *kwan-tow coh-stuh?*
- I'd like _____. :: **Lo vorrei** _____. :: *Yo vohr-ay* _____.
- 1, 2, 3, 4, 5, half-kilo :: **Uno, due, tre, quattro, cinque, mezzo chilo** :: *oo-noh, doo-eh, treh, kwaht-troh, cheen-kweh, meh-dso key-low.*

# 2

# When to Go

F ew other cities on Earth boast an influence as enduring as *la Bella Roma*. Whether you're an art lover, a history buff or a foodie, the memories you'll make on a trip to *la Città Eterna* will linger in your mind for a lifetime.

Everyone wants to see Rome. But I'm often asked when's the "best" time to visit Rome, the Eternal City. It depends, for reasons I go into below. But read on until the end to learn which months I consider the best time to visit Rome.

## Weather

A comfortable Mediterranean climate blesses Rome year-round. Albeit, one that's growing much hotter. Summers are hot and dry, while winters are cool but not bone-chillingly cold.

In spring season (March through May), the temperatures range between lows of 40°F and highs of 70°F. Summer temperatures in June, July and August average around 85°F. However, it's not too humid with comfortable nighttime temperatures. From September to November, average highs fall from the mid-70s to the 60s and rainy days become more common. Last, expect temps between 35°F and 50°F in the winter months.

## Festivals

It should come as no surprise that the two most important days in the Catholic faith (i.e. Christmas and Easter) are also the busiest times in Rome. Don't mind crowds and want to experience the holiday season in Rome? Then consider visiting during these Christian holidays.

Interestingly, many tourism experts now claim that the weeks before and after Easter are more popular than Easter itself. Perhaps foreign tourists figure they'll "miss the crowds" so long as they avoid Easter Sunday. Whatever the reason, keep this tidbit in mind when planning an Easter retreat to Rome.

Religious festivities are central to Rome's identity. But there are many secular events, too. For instance, avid runners should book their trip during Rome's annual marathon that takes place every April.

Classical music lovers will appreciate the Opera at Caracalla. This music festival takes place under the stars at the wondrous Baths of Caracalla every July and August. The venue itself will give you goosebumps. Plus, it features the world's finest operatic performers.

Finally, for party-seekers, consider visiting Rome during Carnival season before Ash Wednesday. While it's no Venice, Rome's Carnival season is just as thrilling. If you're in Rome in March or April, be sure to watch the opening parade on the Via del Corso. Eat tasty treats like fried *castagnole* and take in all the comedic street performances in various piazzas.

## Tourism

The busiest times in Rome are the summer months, especially July and August. While tourists flock to Rome during these months, many Romans flee for their own holidays. You'll find many restaurants and shops are closed in August.

Late autumn and most of the winter (excluding Christmas) are the slowest times for visitors to Rome. While you will have to wear a jacket and long pants during these months, you'll also experience less tourism traffic and reduced rates on hotel rooms.

While springtime rates on hotels aren't as cheap as they are in the winter, the heat is nowhere near as oppressive as the summer. And there won't be quite as many hordes of tourists (except for Holy Week and Easter).

## When I Go to Rome

As long as you avoid July and August, you'll enjoy *la dolce vita* in a comfortable and less-crowded Rome. May, September and October are exceptional times to visit Rome. These are my favorite months. You'll enjoy milder temperatures and reduced crowds. Also, you'll find a better selection of hotels and restaurants. Some will even offer reduced rates come October.

# 3

# Rome Recon

After setting your travel dates, it's time to do some reconnaissance. As your departure date nears, find out what's going on in Rome. Research all the museums, monuments and attractions you want to see. Find out if any of them are closed or have reduced hours. Read up on events and labor strikes. What's the political temperature in Rome? Will there be protests? Parades? How about national holidays? For English-language news from Italy, I start at TheLocal.it and broaden from there with Google searches in both English and Italian (using translation mode, of course).

## Museum Hours

Rome's museums notoriously change hours seasonally and completely out-of-the-blue. Never assume the operating hours in this book apply to your trip. Always double-check.

## Closures & Scaffolding

Renovations happen. In fact, they happen more or less continuously when a city's over 2,000 years old. There's nothing you can do but prepare for it. Research all the museums, monuments and attractions you want to see. Find out if any of them are closed or undergoing major restoration work that might impact your perfect Instagram photo.

## Mondays

Does your trip include a Monday? This is Rome's rest day. Restaurants, museums and attractions close. So do a lot of restaurants. Earmark Mondays for shopping, visiting parks and relaxing.

## Unrest

Labour strikes? Political protests? Check ahead to see if you can expect any major service disruptions from strikes or protests. And, if so, find out where the unrest will happen and plan on steering well clear of that area.

## Festivities, Holidays & Events

Will you be in town for a parade? Major soccer match? How about a national or religious holiday? Just like a labor strike, major events will affect your stay by limiting transportation options, increasing traffic and boosting hotel rates. Conversely, you might have one hell of a fun time during major festivities.

## Links

WEBSITE: thelocal.it

# 4

## Where to Stay

I n chapter two, you read about the best and worst times to visit Rome. Now it's time to look at where to stay on your trip. Rome is a sprawling city. I don't pretend to know it as well as residents or natives. That said, I take great pride in exploring the best neighborhoods for travelers.

In this chapter, I'll provide an overview of my favorite places to bed down in Rome. But first, a few general tips when evaluating your options:

- Air conditioning is pretty much a requirement May through September.
- Airbnb has decent inventory in Rome, especially in Monti, northern Rome and the Pantheon area.
- Hotels reduce their prices by as much as 40% in August and January.
- Book 2-3 months in advance if traveling April to June or September to October.
- While Google Maps and sites like Booking.com are a great way to discover hotels, you can save money by booking

directly with the hotel. Sometimes this means calling or emailing if the hotel doesn't have an online booking function.

· In terms of price and proximity to public transportation, the area west of Termini Station can't be beat. Look on and around Via Firenze.

· Don't judge a hotel off a single recommendation, be it an online user review or a guidebook suggestion. Instead, find something that receives strong reviews from online users and appears in one or two guidebooks.

Ready to find a basecamp in Rome?

## Monti

I'm a sucker for staying in the old city centers of Europe. I like walking to the top sights and strolling the cobblestones early in the morning and after dark. This is especially true in Rome, where the ancient ruins cast an irresistible spell. Therefore, in Rome, I look first in the Centro Storico, specifically the Monti neighborhood. You'll find lots of lodging options around Via Panisperna and Via Cavour.

## Tridente

In northern Rome, hotel-rich Tridente, so called because its three main roads form a trident shape, sits immediately west of Villa Borghese. Look for hotels around Piazza del Popolo and further south along those main thoroughfares, Via di Ripetta, Via del Corso and Via del Babuino.

## Trastevere

Charming Trastevere is filled with small ivy-draped lanes that curl away from an atmospheric central square, Piazza di Santa Maria. You can find clusters of hotels around Via dei Salumi in eastern Trastevere and in the south around Via Ippolito Nievo. Stay south of Viale Trastevere for better restaurants and quieter hotels.

# 5 Killer Apps

L et's talk apps. And I don't mean *tapas*! Unfortunately, that's for another book. Nope, I'm talking about mobile apps for your phone. Specifically, apps for Rome travelers.

Now, using your phone while traveling is inevitable. But try to minimize its use by organizing apps and digital documents. Before every European trip, I save apps in a specifically labeled home-screen folder. The collection ranges considerably depending on where I'm going. I always use Google Maps and Translate. Those are a given. But I also research and download apps tailored to my destination. And when in Rome, these are the apps I download.

## 1. Italian Food Decoder

They designed this 5-star rated app with foodies in mind. Its cost of $4.99 gets you access to explanations for over 6,00 Italian food words that will help you navigate Italian menus. Specifically, this app helps tackle the wide variety of food words used in the various regions of Italy so you'll always know exactly what you're ordering with just a simple search. You can also find links to recipes and Italian food festivals.

- iTunes: apple.co/2L1Ypuh
- Google Play: bit.ly/2GKOS6Z

## 2. Drinking Fountain Finder

If you're worried about getting dehydrated while touring Rome, this free 4-star rated app will quench your thirst. With this app, all you need to do is open its built-in map and zero in on your location. The map will then mark all the public drinking fountains in the vicinity and guide you to a refreshing drink of water. The map is remarkably comprehensive, so you never have to worry about getting too thirsty.

- iTunes: apple.co/2VwaBYa

## 3. Probus Rome

This free 3.5-star rated app will help you tour Rome via bus. The app locates nearby bus stops and ticket sellers so you can easily hop aboard wherever you are. You can use the app to view the routes of specific buses so you know exactly where you're headed. The app even provides approximate arrival times and real-time travel news to keep you up-to-date. However, you will need an Internet connection to search its 8,600 bus stops.

- iTunes: apple.co/2UFa2qv
- Google Play: bit.ly/2IW1tpe

## 4. MiC Roma

For museum-lovers, this free 3.5-star rated app is a must-download. The app gathers information on 20 of Rome's most-popular museums. You can easily research current exhibits, events and galleries. The app also provides information on timetables and ticket prices. And the built-in map can help you navigate to your museum of choice easily.

- iTunes: apple.co/2UJMKQE
- Google Play: bit.ly/2W4lTzT

## 5. Time Travel Rome

I saved the best for last. One of the most appealing things about Rome is its rich history. This app, rated 4.4 stars and free with available in-app purchases, brings that history to life. Specifically, the built-in map function shows you what important locations used to exist exactly where you're standing. You can search for places such as tombs, theaters and monuments and read detailed historical information about each site. You can even find links to ancient texts that mention a particular site.

- iTunes: apple.co/2L3ODIe
- Google Play: bit.ly/2XGVwkb

# 6

# Upon Arrival

S o, there you are: You've arrived in Rome, ready to explore the Eternal City. Ready to embark on the vacation of a lifetime. Except... you're not in Rome. You're some 20 miles from the city. Twenty cursed miles from the Colosseum, Vatican City and all the *cacio e pepe* you can eat. What now?

If you're flying from North America, then chances are you'll land at the super-busy Fiumicino International Airport (FCO). As mentioned, FCO is 20 miles from the heart of Rome and offers travelers three main ways to get into the city: trains, buses and taxis. Well, you could rent a car and drive into Rome. But do you want to deal with feisty Italian drivers on foreign roads... during rush hour? While jet-lagged? Yeah, I didn't think so.

Before choosing how you will get into Rome's center, however, it's important to stop by one of FCO's ATMs to pick up some euros if you have none. No matter how you get into Rome proper, you will need those euros to do it. Also, keep in mind you can pre-purchase train or bus tickets online. Although neither is necessary.

## Is Express Less Stress?

Let's start with Sheldon Cooper's preferred mode of transport: trains! The main advantage with taking one of FCO's two trains is that you avoid the risk of waiting in traffic. This is beneficial if you're arriving in Rome during rush hour. On the flip-side, train travel isn't the cheapest option and it could be a hassle if you're burdened with a ton of luggage.

Choose from the gleaming Leonardo Express or the slower FL1 train. Look for the "Stazione/Railway Station" signs with obvious train icons. You can purchase tickets for both trains at either an automated "*biglietteria*" ticket machine (with an English-language option), ticket window (often with lines) or a newsstand near the train station beside Terminal 1. I recommend using the *biglietteria*. Even though the machines make you pick a time, your ticket is valid for all departure times.

The Leonardo Express line will zip you straight to Rome's central Termini Station in about 30 minutes. And in style: All seats are first-class. Unfortunately for your wallet, these tickets are a tad pricey at €14 per person. At least kids 12 and under ride free. Express trains depart 2-4 times an hour. Remember to get your tickets stamped for validation from the smaller, gray-and-green machines before boarding the train.

If you need not stop in Termini or don't mind connecting via metro, then consider hopping on the FL1 (formerly, FR1). This train makes stops at the following peripheral stations popular with travelers: Trastevere, Ostiense and Tiburtina. So, if your hotel is near any of these areas, the FL1 line is a better choice than the express. Plus, the FL1 is doggone cheap. One-way tickets for this train will cost you about €8. FL1 trains depart every 15 minutes all daylong, except on Sundays or holidays when they run every 30 minutes. Just beware pickpockets frequent this line.

## The Cheapest Way

At the time of publication, four bus companies offered transportation from FCO to Termini. Two of the most respected are SIT and Terravision. All buses have plenty of luggage storage underneath seats and refreshing A/C. The best feature of using a bus is that it's super affordable: Only €6 per person. Just prepare yourself to wait longer to get into Rome, especially if you get caught in traffic. Usually, a bus ride to Termini will take from 45 to 65 minutes. But like taxis and rental cars, buses remain subject to the crazed Roman traffic. Sometimes the bus will take closer to two hours. Yikes.

## The Price of Convenience

Of all three methods of transportation, taxis are both the most convenient and the most expensive. Taxis will bring you straight to your hotel. But that fixed rate of €48 (plus an additional €1 for each piece of luggage) will put a big dent in your travel budget.

Official Roman taxis are white with the "Roma Capitale" logo on the side. You should also see the car's license number and the fixed rates from FCO listed on the side doors. Airport authorities mandate all taxis at FCO must wait outside the Terminal 1 and Terminal 3 arrivals areas. Please don't get in a cab that's waiting outside of these areas because they're most likely unlicensed.

If a driver is giving you a hard time about the €48 price, then you know you're being conned. Either call Rome's official taxi department at +39 06 3570, complain to the taxi-stand attendant or wait for a more honest cab driver in an officially marked taxi.

## Links

WEBSITES:

- Leonardo Express: bit.ly/2XLbwlk
- Terravision: bit.ly/2GxPziC
- SIT: sitbusshuttle.com/en

# 7

## Staying Unlost

B roken into 15 *"municipios"* and split by the Tiber River, Rome, at its heart, is a collection of villages and neighborhoods that share a landlord. You could spend all day reading about each neighborhood, plotting their borders and figuring out their logical intersections. Sounds like fun, right? Instead, I've lumped those neighborhoods together into groups centered on major monuments and attractions.

Realize this is not an exhaustive list. Later on in this book, I will dive into specific neighborhoods. But for orientation, I present the major districts of Rome going from north to south.

### Northern Rome

Comprising everything north of the Piazza Venezia and east of the Tiber, Northern Rome is Borghese territory, the gardens and museum. Both of which are the reasons to come here. It's best reached by Metro.

## Pantheon Neighborhood

This area features—surprise—the Pantheon, but also the Campo de' Fiori and Piazza Navona. This is the pulsating heart of Rome, home to tons of restaurants, bars, cafes, shops and outdoor monuments like the Spanish Steps and Trevi Fountain.

## Ancient Core

Encompassing major ruins like the Colosseum and neighborhoods like Monti and parts of the Centro Storico, the Ancient Core is where ancient Romans built their mightiest buildings. The Ancient Core is wedged between the Tiber River and Northern, Eastern and Southern Rome.

## Eastern Rome

Home to a bunch of churches, Eastern Rome is a transportation hub for travelers. The reason: Termini Station. Chances are, unless you're on a Catholic pilgrimage, connecting through Termini Station is the only reason you'll come here.

## Vatican City

On the west side of the Tiber River, this independent city-state does its own Catholic thing. This is not an area know for great restaurants or outdoor monuments. Instead, come here for its three premier sights: St. Peter's Basilica, Sistine Chapel and the Vatican Museums.

## Trastevere & Monteverde

South of the Vatican, these two neighborhoods get the "chapter treatment" later in this book. So I won't say much more than they're a lovely respite from "tourist" Rome.

## Southern Rome

The Appian Way, Testaccio and a bunch of catacombs draw travelers to this area. With solid public transportation, it's an out-of-the-way area to stay when searching for hotels. We shall see how long that lasts.

Now, go do your own virtual exploration. Jump on Google maps: Find and save hotels, Airbnb apartments, attractions, restaurants, parks, monuments and museums. Explore various neighborhoods at street level using the satellite option. Save it all to your own, customized map of Rome. Download it to your phone for offline use and, presto, you'll stay unlost in Rome.

# 8

# Safety Meeting

The question inevitably arises: Is Rome safe? The answer is an unequivocal yes. Yes, Rome is safe for tourists.

That said, about the only crime you can and should expect is petty, that of the pickpocketing and scam varieties. In fact, you have a far greater chance of losing your valuables than your life. Homicide rates in Rome are less than 1 per 100,000 residents, which is far lower than most American cities of comparable size. Muggings, scams and pickpocketing, however, remain a real threat. Be vigilant in crowded areas like the Termini Station, Trevi Fountain, on the Metro or on bus #64.

To reduce your chances of becoming a victim of petty theft, follow a few of these common-sense tips:

- Invest in a slash-proof, RFID-blocking bag or document holder.
- Never keep your valuables in unsecured pockets.
- Avoid traveling alone at night.
- Make photocopies of important documents (e.g. passport,

driver's license).
- Don't dress like an obvious tourist.
- Be wary of strangers or groups of teens who approach you at popular tourist sights.

If you're unfortunate enough to encounter a pickpocket, then scream out these three words: "*Aiuto, al ladro*," which translates to, "Help, a thief!"

## After Sundown

Like anywhere else on Earth, crime in Rome is more prevalent at night than during the day. Try your best to avoid dimly lit areas such as Termini Station and Piazza Vittorio after the sun goes down. Although Rome is safe for solo tourists, it's always a better idea to walk with at least one companion.

## Crossing the Street

For most travelers, crossing the street represents the biggest safety threat of your trip. It's nothing to fear. Just remember a few key tips before crossing Rome's wide boulevards, traffic-heavy streets and tangled old alleyways:

- Use caution. Look both ways for cars, scooters, bikes and buses.
- Obey pedestrian-crossing signals. Just like traffic lights in North America: Red means don't stop, don't go. Green means go. And yellow means you'd better hustle if you're still crossing or wait for the next green if you haven't left the sidewalk.

- Cross in a group when possible, even if it means keeping stride with locals and breaking that previous tip.

## Safety Services for Tourists

Traveling to Rome soon? Take a moment right now to put this number into your mobile phone: 113. Dialing 113 will put you in touch with the Roman Police Department and is suitable for all major emergencies. It's like our 911. If you need an ambulance, however, then you should call 118 instead.

To file a theft report, you must visit a nearby police station within 24 hours of the crime. While the police most likely won't apprehend the thief or retrieve your belongings, this document is very important for insurance and reimbursement purposes.

The Nuovo Regina Margherita Hospital in Rome's trendy Trastevere district offers a very helpful 24-hour tourist clinic. On the positive side, even if you end up sick or injured during your stay, you'll receive treatment in an ancient monastery. One of the few non-crowded (hopefully) Roman attractions!

## Soccer Safety

Romans are passionate about their soccer. So are fans of other teams. Unfortunately, sometimes this passion turns into violent clashes between diehard fans of opposing teams. And Rome has two major soccer teams (A.S. Roma and S.S. Lazio), further dividing the city's soccer lovers. You might avoid professing allegiances until you're familiar with Rome's soccer rivalry and Serie A (Italy's top-tier professional league). Especially on game days.

## Links

WEBSITE: Nuovo Regina Margherita Hospital: bit.ly/2UU4Unz

GOOGLE MAP: NRM Hospital: goo.gl/maps/123LgtJ8sD12

# 9

# The WiFi Hunt

I n 2017, the Italian government took a giant leap into the 21st century. They unveiled a free mobile app that allows access to thousands of WiFi hotspots throughout the country. And get this: Sometimes it works!

Called "Italia WiFi," the app is available on Android and Apple devices. Politicians claim the app works on about 28,000 hotspots throughout the nation. But you shouldn't set your expectations too high. Let's get real: Italy isn't Silicon Valley. Italy's average internet speed ranks toward the bottom when compared with other European nations. You might experience connectivity issues and/or long lag times when using this app. But, hey, it's free to download. So try it.

If internet access is a big deal to you, then you should check whether your hotel offers high-speed WiFi before booking your trip. Please note: Not all hotels have WiFi. Plus, most hotels will charge an extra fee for it. Your best bet for getting free and fast—um, well at least faster—WiFi is to book an Airbnb. As always, check out the reviews for whatever Airbnb you're interested in and look under the "Details" tab to see if they offer

WiFi.

While coworker culture is not widespread, Rome's coworking scene is growing. You shouldn't have great difficulty hunting down cafes, bars and restaurants that cater to digital nomads. Although you could find WiFi-friendly establishments all over Rome, your best bet is to try the trendy Trastevere first. Since Trastevere is home to the American University campus, it makes sense that many of the cafes here cater to internet addicts (AKA grad students). If you can't find a suitable WiFi spot in Trastevere, then the next best place to explore is the touristy Centro Storico. Of course, you could always ask your hotel concierge to point you toward a good WiFi-enabled cafe.

## Links

WEBSITES:

- Italia WiFi for Apple: apple.co/2PwqisV
- Italia WiFi for Google Play/Android: bit.ly/2W1EaxX

# 10

# Cash is King

Italy, like most countries in the European Union, uses the euro (€). Europeans put the euro sign after the amount and use a comma where North Americans use the decimal point. For example, a 4.50-euro coffee gets written as 4,50€. But here's where it gets a little convoluted: When written in English, we place the euro sign before the amount. So this little book adheres to that usage guideline.

Cash is still king in Rome—especially at the small, family run establishments favored by me and listed in this book. Even big chains expect shoppers to use cash for small purchases. Italians reserve the plastic for large transactions. Many small hotels and some travel agencies offer a 5-10% discount for cash payment. Plan to use cash for most non-restaurant meals and carry several small bills because...

Surprise! Italian shop clerks prefer exact change or a round number close to the total so they don't have to fuss with breaking euros. Being asked by clerks for exact change or a rounder sum can surprise—to Americans especially, where the customer can do no wrong and expect businesses to bend over backwards to accommodate customers. But Romans prefer practicality (at least in making change... Women's shoes? Not so much.). Phew, that's a long-winded way of saying it's good form to carry small bills, an array of change and one-euro coins.

Your ATM card should work just fine in Rome. ATMs are the best way to withdraw cash—the rates and fees are far better than doing currency exchange or using traveler's checks. Since you have a daily withdrawal limit and you don't want to spend your first moments in Rome hunting for an ATM, order euros from your bank, usually for no extra charge, several weeks before departure. I use Wells Fargo and like to depart with at least €1,000.

# 11

## Beat the Heat

There's no getting around it. In Rome in summer, you will sweat. From May to August, daytime highs routinely hit the lower 90s°F and even 100°F. On top of the sun and humidity, you also have to factor in the aggravation of tourist hordes getting in your way. Summer is, remember, the height of Rome's tourism season.

The worst time to be walking outside is between noon and 3PM when the sun is at its highest. Once you feel that Mediterranean heat for yourself, you'll understand why so many Romans take a siesta after lunch. Consider taking a break of your own mid-day so you'll feel refreshed for an evening stroll (AKA "passeggiata") when temps fall. Please ensure whatever hotel you're staying at has a good AC system before booking your room.

## What to Wear

Choosing your clothes carefully can help you feel refreshed even on the warmest of Roman days. Opt for lightweight and breathable clothing, especially linen. A few cooling fashion accessories you should include in your wardrobe include a shady hat and protective sunglasses. Also, don't forget to apply sunscreen every day to avoid sunburn. For those who are feeling the heat, purchase a handy hand fan at one of the many Roman tourist boutiques.

## Chillax in Catacombs & Churches

Definitely don't schedule the Spanish Steps for mid-afternoon! If you want to continue sightseeing in the hottest part of the day, find some way to get out of the sun. Thankfully, Rome's many churches and catacombs offer a welcome respite from the searing sunlight.

Some of Rome's best catacombs include the Catacombs of Priscilla, Catacombs of San Sebastiano and the Catacombs of Callixtus. For churches, there's always St. Peter's Basilica or the Pantheon. Want to beat the crowds and the heat? Try visiting lesser-known churches like the Basilica di Santa Maria Maggiore, Santa Maria Sopra Minerva and the Basilica di San Pietro in Vincoli. If you plan on visiting churches, please be sure to dress modestly (that means cover your shoulders and knees).

## Water & Gelato

The ancient Romans were master engineers, especially with aqueducts. Thirsty tourists and locals still enjoy the water from Rome's many historic fountains. Avoid the ridiculous prices for bottled water by carrying an empty container and filling it up at one of Rome's plentiful public fountains (the Forum alone has three).

Besides staying hydrated, there's no more Roman way to cool off than by eating a cup (or two) of your favorite gelato. Don't worry about counting calories. When in Rome, eat plenty of gelato!

# 12

# Public Transportation

**G**ood news travelers: Getting around the Eternal City ain't hard at all. With this handy guide, you'll jump from Metro to bus to Ancient Roman ruins with nary a hassle. Let's go!

First, let's review the basics. Rome's public-transportation network includes two Metro lines (with a partially operational third under construction through 2022), a tangle of bus routes and a half-dozen trams. One organization, ATAC, manages everything. Therefore, you can use the same tickets on any mode of transportation. Speaking of tickets, you must purchase them before riding. Even on buses, drivers don't sell tickets. Check tobacco shops, newsstands or the ubiquitous gray ticket machines at bus stops and Metro stations. Last, do yourself a favor and visit ATAC's website at least once before traveling to Rome so you have a good sense of where all these services go.

## Ticket Options

There are four major ticket options on Rome's ATAC public transportation system. The best value for tourists is the BIT ticket, which allows you 75 minutes' access on Rome's public transport for only €1.50. Your 75-minute adventure begins after you validate your BIT ticket for the first time, so you could stack up on these bad boys well in advance. One annoying caveat with the BIT ticket is that it allows only one ride on the Metro.

ATAC also sells the BIG day pass, the BTI 3-day pass and the CIS week pass. These are each priced at €6, €16.50, €24, respectively. Note: Each pass begins upon validation and ends at midnight on the final day specified. This means if you validate your BIG pass at 5PM, then it will end at 12AM that day instead of 5PM the next day.

You can pick up any of these tickets on touchscreen machines at most Metro stations, bus stops, newsstands and tobacco shops.

## Roma Pass & Public Transportation

If you're looking into tourist passes, then consider investing in a Roma Pass. There are two Roma Passes on offer: a 48-hour pass for €28 and a 72-hour pass for €38.50. With either of these passes, you'll enjoy free access to all ATAC public transport for either 48 or 72 hours and dozens of discounts at dozens of tourist sights. Travelers who opt for the 48-hour pass get free access to one Roma Pass-listed museum, whereas the 72-hour pass holder can get into two attractions. You can find much more information about the Roma Pass in chapter 18.

## Pickpocket Express

Rome's mighty bus fleet has 338 lines that dump travelers at over 8,200 stops. All the urban buses are open from 5AM till 6:30AM and night buses run from midnight till about 5AM.

As a visitor, focus your attention on the 40 and 64 lines. Both lines travel out of Termini Station towards the Vatican. But the 40 route only makes nine stops while the 64 makes 18 stops. No matter what line you take, you'll be able to get off near all the major draws, including the Colosseum, central Rome and good old St. Peter's Basilica.

Warning: These touristy bus lines are notorious for petty theft. Locals don't call them the "Pickpocket Express" for nothing!

## It Ain't Tokyo

Compared with Paris and London, Rome's Metro is humble. There are only two major lines on this Metro system, the creatively named Line A (traveling northwest to southeast) and Line B (traveling northeast to south). The partially open Line C comes fully online in 2022.

Although the Rome Metro isn't huge, we have to give it some props for tourist convenience. For example, on Line A, you could get close to the Vatican at Cipro, hop off right by Villa Borghese at Flaminio and arrive a short distance from the Trevi Fountain at Barberini. The most important tourist stop on Line B is the Colosseum. Both Metro lines also make stops in Rome's main transportation hub, Termini Station. The Metro is open between 5:30AM and 11:30PM every day except Fridays and Saturdays when it is open till 1:30AM.

## Hey, Look: Trams!

You can see most of Rome's sights just using the Metro and buses, but there is also a tram service should you need it. While mostly locals use these six tram lines to get around town, they could be useful if you want to see a slice of authentic Roman life. Tram #8 has become popular because of the growing prominence of trendy Trastevere. Trams run from 5:30AM till midnight. Validate tram tickets using the on-board machine.

## Links

WEBSITE: atac.roma.it/index.asp?lingua=ENG

# 13

# Ubers & Taxis

Although it's possible to rely on Rome's public transportation and your own two feet, you can't deny the convenience of Ubers and taxis. Before we get into how to hail a taxi, first let's address everyone's top concern: cost.

First off, both airports have instituted fixed rates for travel into the city center. Travel from Ciampino International Airport to Rome's center will costs €30. From the larger Fiumicino International Airport into Rome, however, you must pay €48. You should also tack on an extra €1 per piece of luggage. If a driver is giving you a hard time about these fixed prices, then you're getting ripped off.

When picking up a taxi in Rome, expect the meter to start at different prices depending on the time of day. For instance, the meter starts at €3 on weekdays between 6-10AM, but it costs €4.50 during those same hours on the weekend. If traveling by taxi between 10PM to 6AM, your taxi's meter will start at €6.50.

The driver's meter will calculate prices depending on how many kilometers they travel at 20-km per hour. The first rate is €1.10 per km, and this continues until your total fee reaches

€11. After that, the fee moves up to €1.30 per km. Once your total reach €13, however, the metered fee will bump up to €1.60 per km.

## How To Hail a Taxi

All official Roman taxis are white with a prominent "*Roma Capitale*" logo and license number listed on the side. While you could hail these taxis from the street, it's far more common to get in a cab at one of the many taxi stands known as "ranks" sprinkled throughout the city. Don't worry, there are plenty of these ranks at all the major tourist draws. Just keep your eyes peeled for the bright orange "taxi" signs.

Need a Roman taxi in a New York minute? Consider calling this official Rome City Council number to send one to your location: +39 060609. If you're at your hotel, you could always ask a concierge for help to hail taxis.

## Is Uber Legit in Rome?

Although city taxi drivers remain none too thrilled, Uber now "operates" a fleet in La Bella Roma. There's just one slight catch: you can only choose from Uber Black, Uber Lux and Uber Van. So, if you don't mind paying extra to ride around Rome in style, open your app and hail an Uber.

## Pro Tip: Avoid During Rush Hour

Just like any other major city, Rome has morning and evening rush hours... and you don't want to get caught up in the madness. The morning rush lasts from about 7AM to 9AM and the evening rush starts at 6PM and lasts till about 8PM. Unless you enjoy sitting in gridlock traffic, we'd advise you to avoid hailing a cab during these times. For a more pleasant travel experience, relax in a Roman caffè during these hours and just watch the craziness pass you by. Or walk.

# 14

# Vatican City vs. Eternal City

S o, there you are: Standing atop St. Peter's Basilica looking out as Rome unfolds beneath you in every direction. Or, wait, maybe that's Vatican City beneath you. Right about now you might wonder, why is the Vatican separate from Rome? First, let's back up: What is the difference between Vatican City and the city of Rome? And how did this difference come to be? Let's find out.

## The Founding of Vatican City

From the 8th through 18th centuries, Italy wasn't a unified nation. Instead, Papal States—territories under the direct rule of the Pope—independent minor kingdoms and city-states ruled different regions, often in competition with one another. However, the Italian unification movement (1815–1871) hoped to consolidate rule of the entire peninsula under one government. In an era when big countries across Western Europe were eating their smaller neighbors, momentum for a single Italy grew.

Vatican City was the only Papal State not seized as part of the unification. The Italian Kingdom even annexed Rome and made it the capital in 1870. From 1870 until 1929, the Pope maintained secular authority over the Vatican. During this time, the Popes overseeing Vatican City asserted that the Italian king had no right to rule Rome. In fact, to avoid looking like they recognized the kings' right to rule, Popes during these years refused to leave the Vatican.

Then, in 1929, the Popes and Italian government forged an agreement called the Lateran Treaty. This agreement established Vatican City as an independent entity within Rome. Although Vatican City has some characteristics of an independent nation, such as the ability to print its own money and maintain its own postal system, it isn't a typical country. For example, no one is ever born with Vatican citizenship. Instead, they issue citizenship only to those with an official purpose. The citizenship of the country comprises three groups: clergy, the Swiss Guard and diplomats.

The rest of Rome is a typical city, serving as capital of the sovereign nation of Italy. And there you have it: Vatican City versus the Eternal City.

But while we're discussing Vatican City...

## Did You Know?

- Vatican City consumes more wine per capita than any other country in the world. Statistics show that a citizen of Vatican City drinks about 74 liters of wine each year.
- Every citizen of Vatican City is Catholic. In fact, Catholic clergy accounts for approximately 72% of the population.
- About 18 million people visit Vatican City each year. Rome,

on the other hand, sees about 12 million tourists each year. Something's fishy here because visitors have to enter Rome to visit the Vatican City. Unless, of course, 6 million tourists a year are entering the Vatican via helicopter...

- The crime rate in Vatican City is low: it sees about 0.87 crimes per capita each year.
- Vatican City owns a telescope in the United States so it can conduct astronomical research without the interference of light pollution from Rome.
- St. Peter's Basilica stands atop a burial ground said to contain St. Peter's body.

## Links

WEBSITE: w2.vatican.va/content/vatican/en.html

GOOGLE MAP: goo.gl/maps/Sfeszv22qDCpsDeS8

# II

# Go » See » Do

*Sightseeing Tips – Museums – Attractions –*
*Monuments – Neighborhoods*

# 15

# One Pass to Rule Them All

I'm a big fan of European city and museum passes. City passes like the Roma Pass save you time, money and make your sightseeing days easier and less stressful. And among European museum passes, the Roma Pass stands out. It offers free admission to your first one or two sights, discounted admission for other sights, line-skipping privileges and free use of public transportation.

## The Benefits

Hate lines? Enjoy saving money? Prefer sightseeing with fewer hassles? The Roma Pass checks all those boxes. With a Roma Pass, visiting Rome's sights becomes easier and cheaper. You'll pay way less than if you bought tickets for each sight. And you'll get to skip the long lines.

Popular sights included on the Roma Pass:

- Colosseum
- Galleria Borghese

- Capitoline Museums
- Castel Sant'Angelo
- Rome National Museums
- Ara Pacis
- Palazzo Valentini
- Ostia Antica (including the train out there)

In addition, you get unlimited use of the in-town buses, Metro and trams. Plus, pass holders receive a cool and useful fold-out map of the city that will make a great keepsake for your trip. I still have all of mine!

However, keep in mind the pass doesn't include several popular attractions:

- Vatican Museums
- Domus Aurea
- Night visits to the Colosseum
- Viaggio nei Fori
- Leonardo Express train from Fiumicino into Rome Termini (i.e., the train from the airport to the city center)

The pass comes in two forms:

1. The 48-hour pass includes one free sight.
2. The 72-hour pass includes two free sights.

Unless you're spending your entire trip inside Vatican City, buying a Roma Pass is an easy decision. So that leaves just one question...

## How to Buy It

There are a lot of purchase options, including online and at the sights included in the pass. However, the better option is to buy a pass at a subway ticket office, tourist office or tobacco shop. You can buy one at all Trenitalia (Italy's national railway) ticket offices.

Only adults need a Roma Pass. Kids under 18 gain free entry to national museums and sights and can skip the line alongside their pass-wielding parents. However, you will need to buy transit tickets for anyone 10 years and older.

The pass activates the first time you use it. Whenever you visit one of the included sights, just present your pass. On a bus or the Metro, place the card on the black circle of the yellow reader to ride for free.

## Pro Tips

To ensure you receive your money's worth, use your pass at the two most-expensive sights first: the Colosseum and Capitoline Museums.

Also, don't be afraid to get aggressive! One of the most exciting benefits of the Roma Pass is skipping lines, so push to the front of the line at crowded sights with your Roma Pass in-hand and visible.

## Reservations

For Roma Pass holders, reservations are now mandatory at the Colosseum. There are three ways to book: by phone, online and at the Roman Forum ticket counter.

A €2 booking fee applies to all reservations made by phone or online. To reserve, call +06 39967575 or go to the website. The online booking or call center will issue a voucher. Bring the voucher and Roma Pass to the "Reserved" counter at the Roman Forum ticket offices. They'll issue you a receipt showing your entry time and that you paid or you are using one of your free admissions. Use this and your Roma Pass to enter at the appointed time. Does this sound complicated or what? Welcome to Italy!

You can also reserve a time day-of at the Roman Forum–Palatine tickets offices. Here, there is no booking fee. The ticket office will issue your voucher with an admission time on the same day. But this is subject to availability. During busy tourism times, eat the booking fee and reserve online.

For reservations to the Borghese Gallery and/or Domus Romane/Palazzo Valentini, call +39 06 32810 or email. There is no booking fee if the Borghese is one of your free entrances. Otherwise, they will add a €2 reservation fee to the reduced-entry price.

## Links

WEBSITES:

- Roma Pass: romapass.it/en/home
- Colosseum: bit.ly/2DIgyrd
- Borghese (email): info@tosc.it

# 16

# Do You Have a Reservation? Part 1

As we left St. Peter's Square in Vatican City one searing June morning en route to the Vatican Museums, we ran smack into a congregation of tourists milling about. I assumed a tour bus had just dropped off, and they were waiting for their tour guide. But circumventing the bulbous crowd, we realized it wasn't a tour group at all, but the end of a long line.

"It can't be," I muttered to my wife. "This can't be the line to the Vatican Museums. We're still 10 minutes away." But it could and it was. The line, which also switchbacks a half-dozen times at the museums' entrance, stretched all along Vatican City's wall to just past the gated Porta Sant'Anna. I measured the distance in Google Maps: a half-mile. But there'd be no half-mile wait in the 90-degree heat for us — we had booked our tickets in advance.

Lines. Lines. Lines. If you don't plan, then your impression of Rome's top sights will be just that: Lines all day. Don't waste hours of your precious sightseeing time standing around waiting. Instead, buy a Roma Pass and reserve ahead at these three key attractions: the Vatican Museums (recommended),

Colosseum (recommended) and Borghese Gallery (required).

## The Vatican Museums

Home to the Sistine Chapel, Raphael Rooms and Laocoön, is it any wonder there's always a huge line? Sure, you could wait in line for hours to get inside these museums... but why? You must pay a little extra to skip the line with an online reservation, but it's well worth it. Exploring these massive museums is a better way to spend two hours than waiting in line. Plus, as you stride past that excruciatingly long line, filled with dour, sweaty faces, you'll feel like a real travel pro as you proudly clutch your pre-booked ticket. The booking fee will prove to be the best €4 you'll spend in Rome.

On the Vatican Museums' website, choose the "Full entry ticket Skip the Line," which goes on sale 90 days in advance. You must choose a specific time and date. Please note, you can't use your Roma Pass to visit the Vatican Museums.

A word of advice: The Vatican Museums offer free access on the last Sunday of every month. So expect extra crazy crowds on these days.

## Cutting the Colosseum Line

There's no better symbol of Rome's gory glory than the Colosseum. Even though the gladiators are long gone, you'll still find a crowd of tourists clamoring to get inside the Flavian Amphitheater. The Colosseum can accommodate 3,000 visitors at a time. That sounds like a lot. But, relative to the amount of tourists who show up every day, it's not. So prepare yourself to fiddle on your iPhone for a few hours if you didn't pre-book skip-the-line tickets.

Thankfully, buying tickets online up to 90 days in advance couldn't be easier. But don't delay in summer. Go to the website and choose your day and time as soon as you're ready. Be sure to show up at the correct entrance (there are three) at least 30 minutes before your scheduled entry time.

Roma Pass holders can use a special line to get inside the Colosseum, Roman Forum and Palatine Hill. For Roma Pass holders, reservations are now mandatory at the Colosseum. There are three ways to book: by phone, online and at the Roman Forum ticket counter.

## Booking Borghese

The Borghese Gallery, housed in an extravagant 17th-century villa and home to dozens of masterpieces by the likes of Bernini and Canova, is reservation only.

Because of its smaller size, the Borghese Gallery can only hold 360 visitors at a time. You must pay a fee to book your time slot on the Borghese Gallery's online portal. Your ticket will grant you only two hours inside the Borghese Gallery, so please use the restroom beforehand! Plan to arrive at least 30 minutes early with your ticket in-hand.

You can use your Roma Pass for a free or discounted ticket to the Borghese Gallery, but you must arrange a two-hour slot beforehand by phone or email.

## Links

WEBSITE:

- Vatican Museums: bit.ly/2IX79PG
- Colosseum: coopculture.it/en/colosseo-e-shop.cfm
- Borghese Gallery: gebart.it/en/home_en/borghese-gallery-and-museum

GOOGLE MAP:

- Vatican Museums: goo.gl/maps/Gwa9LqNJNex
- Colosseum: goo.gl/maps/dp5SP3iRghn
- Borghese Gallery: goo.gl/maps/3e34b4MT7sE2

# 17

# Beating the Crowds

Travelers love Rome. And for good reason: It's amazing. Food, art, ruins, museums, it's all good here. Well, almost. The crowds? Not so good. In fact, travelers might just be loving Rome to death. In peak season, tourists fill the city's top sights. Mammoth tour buses deposits hundreds of tourists at a time, inundating popular sights like the Colosseum and St. Peter's Basilica by 9AM.

I'm here to help. Now, there's no avoiding crowds completely unless you visit in January. But by following the tips below, you'll stay a step ahead of those pesky tour buses.

- **Make reservations.** Especially for the Vatican Museums. Unless you skipped the last chapter, you've got a handle on this.
- **Buy a Roma Pass.** And use it to skip the line wherever possible. Again, the Roma Pass chapter should have already convinced you of its value.
- **Start your Vatican City day at St. Peter's Basilica at 7AM.** Make an afternoon reservation at the Vatican Museums.

- **Devise a daily sightseeing plan (see next chapter) that groups adjacent attractions logically.** Even if it means not setting everything in stone, follow a general outline that prioritizes crowd-skipping.
- **Go early or late to popular attractions.** For early risers, hit up a church at 7AM since they open first. When sightseeing late, remember museums and monuments stop admitting visitors 30-45 minutes before closing time.
- **Visit outdoor monuments and fountains first thing in the morning.** Tired of seeing churches at 7AM? Mix up your morning routine by taking your coffee to the Spanish Steps, Trevi Fountain, Piazza Navona or another outdoor, ticket-less attraction.
- **Splurge on a guided tour.** Research themed tours like foodie walks or intimate behind-the-scenes tours of major attractions like the Sistine Chapel. Book at least a couple months in advance for high-season travel.
- **When buying combination tickets, always purchase at the less-popular one.** For example, to jump the Colosseum's queue, buy a combo ticket at the Palatine Hill ticket booth. It's just a five-minute stroll away with rarely a line. Then return to the Colosseum.
- **Tour major attractions in reverse.** Most sights, especially museums, have a preferred path they want you to travel. But there's no law mandating it! So, cut to the end of the "tour" and walk it in reverse.

# 18

# The Ultimate Day

Ready to go all out? Or all in? Whatever the saying, this chapter's about how to make the absolute most of your precious days in Rome. Have only a few days? Follow this regiment daily. Have a week? (Bless you, child.) Do this every other day. Just remember the saying, "You can sleep when you're dead."

## Morning

The Ultimate Day is not for sleepy heads. You came here to live it up not sleep. Therefore, hit the streets for a morning stroll at 6AM. The ruins, piazzas, monuments and fountains are no finer than when you're enjoying them with the street sweepers and joggers. Not a gaggle of tourists. Grab breakfast around 6:30AM.

Once 7AM strikes, be at your first attraction of the day: a Roman church. Almost all churches open around 7AM on weekdays. The most obvious church to visit is St. Peter's Cathedral. There are, however, many lesser-known (but insanely gorgeous) churches in Rome. Consider visiting the Basilica of Santa Maria Maggiore near Termini Station. Or the Santa Maria sopra Minerva near the Pantheon for a more intimate church-going experience. Both churches open at 7AM on weekdays.

Side note: You could also replace a church with the Colosseum. The Colosseum usually opens at 8:30AM. This gives you time to sip your cappuccino outside the Colosseum entrance. Enjoy this quiet moment before the tour groups arrive.

After admiring one historic house of worship, it's time to play "dodge the tourists." Seriously, 10AM is peak tour group-craziness hour, so it's best to head to a "hidden gem" attraction during this time of day.

Stroll one of Rome's parks or visit a unique museum. For example, walk through the city's Botanical Garden and then visit the nearby Galleria Corsini. Both are close to the Lgt Gianicolense/Regina Coeli bus stop. Alternatively, you could book a tour of the famous Borghese Gallery for 10AM. This reservation-required museum admits only 360 guests every two hours.


## Afternoon

After all that walking around Rome, it's time to get your foodie-face on. Some of the best places to eat lunch are at Testaccio Market or in the historic Jewish Ghetto. Wherever you go, don't worry about eating like a pig. The next step in our Ultimate Rome Day is to take an epic nap! Or at least relax in a shady and cool space. As Rome swelters under intense afternoon heat, read, nap, play cards in your (hopefully) air-conditioned hotel room or Airbnb for a couple hours.

Since the heat lingers till about 6PM, head to an indoor (or underground, like catacombs) attraction around 4PM. Thankfully, tour groups are wrapping up their adventures by this time. So it's a great idea to tackle one more major attraction. Consider visiting the Pantheon, Castel Sant'Angelo or even the Vatican Museums during this time.

## Evening

Once you're done with your last major sight, join the locals in what's known as a passeggiata. Usually beginning around 6PM, a passeggiata refers to an evening stroll where Romans enjoy the Mediterranean sunset and cooler evening temps. Work your way to one of Rome's great piazzas. Then, sit back at a cafe and people-watch with a pre-dinner drink (AKA an aperitivo).

## Night

By 8PM, be at your dinner destination. Um, you got a reservation beforehand... right? Yeah, do your restaurant research in advance so you don't look like a starving fool at this hour. Sure, you could chance it, but that's risky if you're traveling during the height of tourism season.

Romans eat late into the night, so don't worry about lingering at your restaurant for hours. You've earned it. As a final treat, take a nighttime stroll to see some of Rome's great fountains, monuments and piazzas all bathed in floodlights. Heck, why not grab a little vino (Rome has no open-container laws) or a gelato as you head back to your hotel? When in Rome, right?

# 19

# Going Gratis

There are many ways to save some scratch when traveling. And in an expensive country like Italy every euro counts. So, clever travelers and proud tightwads should incorporate three key saving opportunities into their Rome trip: Free first Sundays, free last Sundays and free for under 18s.

## Free First Sundays... For Now

Seeking the cheapest way to see Rome's top tourist draws? Book your trip during the first Sunday of the month. This takes advantage of Italy's Domenica al Museo, which means "Sunday at the Museum." All state-sponsored museums and archeological sites are free to the public on this one day. Yes, that means sights as iconic as the Colosseum, Roman Forum and Palatine Hill are 100% gratis!

While you could go to popular sights like the Colosseum on this day, think again. It's far wiser to use Domenica al Museo to explore lesser-known and less-crowded sights that are equally stunning. Consider touring the National Museum of Rome, Castel Sant'Angelo, Palazzo Barberini and the Baths of Caracalla. Plus, sights do not offer reservations on first Sundays, making them even more of a zoo.

Unfortunately, the new Italian government has announced it will stop funding Domenica al Museo by the summer of 2019. In Italian politics, that's a lifetime away. Several more governments may come and go in that time span. Instead of doing free first Sundays, the government would like to give attractions more flexibility to hold free days. As with much in Italian politics, details remain scarce. There's still no official word if they will carry this policy out. But it's better to take advantage now if you can.

## Complimentary Vatican Museums

The Vatican Museums are too cool to join the other museums on Domenica al Museo. Though they still dangle a freebie. But instead of the first Sunday, the Vatican Museums open for free on the last Sunday of every month. The Vatican Museums also throw open their doors for free on certain religious holidays. You'd better believe there are humongous crowds on free days.

## Under 18s

If you're young and in Rome, you're in luck. Also: I'm jealous! Most of Rome's state-sponsored museums and archeological sites offer free entry to anyone under the age of 18. Some museums also offer free or discounted access to students between the ages of 18-25, though many restrict this benefit to EU citizens. Regardless, it's worthwhile for students in this age range to carry their school ID card. And remember: Even if the sight you want to visit is free for your age bracket, you still might have to or want to reserve your spot in advance.

# 20

# Dress for Success

Stylish yet comfortable. That's my advice on dressing for Rome. Rome, like most big cities in the US and Europe, is fashion-forward. And the more you dress like a local, the better you'll fit in. However, as a sightseer, I recommend balancing style with comfort, especially during sweltering summer trips. Travelers must also plan for conservative dress codes in churches, which prohibit exposed thighs and shoulders. Don't piss off God (or, rather, his Earthly minders). But also stay stylish and comfortable while traveling Rome with these tips.

## Modesty in Churches

Visiting the Eternal City's historic churches is a lifelong thrill. Keep in mind, though, that these religious sights have strict dress codes. And they enforce them. This is true for the major attractions like the Pantheon and throughout Vatican City, namely St. Peter's Basilica.

When picking out clothes to wear to churches, just remember

that modesty is key. Wear long pants and clothing that covers your shoulders and thighs. Jeans are fine, but they should have no rips, grime or "fashionable" tears in them. Keep your shoulders and knees covered at all times.

Women can get away with wearing capris, skirts, or dresses, so long as they extend below the knees. Shorts, however, remain verboten in most Roman churches. Ladies (or men) wearing tank tops must cover their shoulders with something like a large, non-transparent scarf, sarong or a shawl. Consider planning the days you wish to visit religious sights ahead of time so you'll know when to prioritize modest attire.

## Light & Bright

Fashion experts often explain Italian fashion by contrasting it with the French. While black and understated colors are the norm in Paris, Italians favor lighter colors in their wardrobe. These lighter colors have a practical purpose: They reflect the intense Roman sun. When in Rome, dress like the Romans by favoring a lighter-colored wardrobe. Wearing breathable clothing is a must on hot summer days as you're hiking around attractions like Palatine Hill and the Roman Forum.

## Don't Look Like a Tourist

Unfortunately, there's a lot of petty crime in the Italian capital. Looking like an obvious tourist is the fastest way to get pick-pocketed. So, when packing up your clothing, always ask yourself whether your wardrobe screams "clueless tourist."

A few pointers: Eschew clothes with prominent logos, especially ones from your home country. You should also avoid wearing baseball hats, fanny packs, cargo shorts and synthetic sportswear or "athleisure" wear. Instead, pick up a locally made fedora or sun hat, use a hidden money belt and stick to clothes made from denim, linen, leather, cotton and other natural materials. Finally, let me drive home this point: You will scream obvious American tourist if you wear Under Armour clothing. This abhorrent clothing line should stay where it belongs—the gym. Leave the Under Armour at home. Or, better yet, burn your Under Armour now.

As for footwear, it's best to wear semi-formal shoes (e.g. leather or suede) that fit you well, hold up to lots of walking and look nice enough for an evening out. I'm darn loyal to the Ecco brand. Lightweight slip-on shoes are popular as are sturdy, leather sandals. Avoid tennis shoes and plastic flip-flops.

# 21

# The Ruins Circuit

Unless you're a Catholic pilgrim or a history-hating foodie, this is why you're here: To see Roman ruins. Good news, traveler: The ancient Romans were thoughtful enough to group their wonderful ruins next to each other. That makes it easy to explore a bunch of Roman ruins in a one-day walking circuit.

Now, several wonderful ruins sit outside this circuit. I'm not suggesting you skip them. It's just that, geographically, they make little sense to include in this ancient-core walk. And there are lesser ruins found all along this route I've omitted to keep a focus on the heavy hitters. But check them out, too. You can't miss them.

This tour starts at the Colosseum and ends at the Pantheon. Each ruin includes a Google Map links and a brief description.

1. **Colosseum**: goo.gl/maps/6ZqzS5pK1Cwo5WPx5

Beginning in 80 AD, the Colosseum hosted gladiator exhibitions, dramatic reenactments of historic battles and fights between exotic animals.

2. **Arch of Constantine**: goo.gl/maps/GgqQDWakDLkpRrNT9
Commemorating Constantine I's victory over Maxentius at the Battle of Milvian Bridge in 312, this is Rome's largest triumphal arch.

3. **Palatine Hill**: goo.gl/maps/QrQ81dMrZnVrxSyC9
With evidence of human habitation since the 10th-century BC, this is where Rome began. (Detour downhill to the west for a look at the Circus Maximus.)

4. **Roman Forum**: goo.gl/maps/pEjcC4sqbX21XKEw5
Public speeches, triumphant parades, markets, criminal trials, gladiator matches, for centuries the Roman Forum served as Rome's beating heart.

5. **Forum Vespasian (Temple of Peace)**: goo.gl/maps/YGvAPi-aVTdgHKEFx7
Dedicated to Emperor Vespasian's sacking of Jerusalem, the temple once held war booty collected by the Roman Army.

6. **Marcello Theater**: goo.gl/maps/4janU3BVqZkfqYAc6
The "Jewish Colosseum" was conceived of by Julius Caesar and brought to fruition by Augustus in 12 BC.

7. **Forum of Caesar**: goo.gl/maps/Zycb8H96eTPkyCmK7
Originally envisioned as an extension of the Roman Forum, Caesar forced the Senate to meet him here under a temple dedicated to... himself.

8. **Forum of Augustus**: goo.gl/maps/BeBVcMSfiLg7TKEm7
Built to honor the god Mars and provide another public forum,

Augustus used the forum to spread propaganda linking himself to the gods.

9. **Forum of Trajan**: goo.gl/maps/FHuyL6yfdJMsthRY9
Adjacent to Trajan's Market and built using the spoils of war from the conquest of Dacia, this was ancient Rome's last public forum.

10. **Trajan's Market**: goo.gl/maps/RbSnd1qG2QxJo7qr7
The world's oldest shopping mall has been restored and offers a look at ancient life.

11. **Pantheon**: goo.gl/maps/5N6iwLY7CResarW2A
Far from a "ruin," the Pantheon is regarded as Rome's most-intact ancient building.

# 22

# Climbing St. Peter's

Welcome to the most-famous church in Christendom, St. Peter's Basilica. Drawing pilgrims and tourists from across the globe, St. Peter's Basilica is the second-largest church in the world. It can hold over 60,000 worshippers at once. The interior is fascinating, filled with priceless sculptures, paintings and frescoes. Plus, the immense scale of everything is humbling. But as wondrous as the interior is, I find climbing the dome an even more magical experience.

The dome is the symbol of the Church of Rome. It's the "beacon" that lures visitors to the heart of Christianity. Started by Michelangelo in 1546, work ceased upon his death in 1564. Fifteen years later, Giacomo della Porta and Domenico Fontana restarted construction and finished in under two years. So, I guess, Michelangelo was a slacker, eh?

## To the Top

Arrive at St. Peter's at 7AM when it opens (remember to "dress for success"). Spend an hour inside then make your way to the dome entrance by 8AM. From inside, turn left when exiting the basilica. Or, if you tackle the dome climb first, turn right after passing through St. Peter's security checkpoint. Either way, follow signs that say "Cupola." Walk through the portico and past the "Holy Door" until you reach the ticket office.

From here, you have 2 options:

1. Climb all the way on foot (551 steps).

2. Take the elevator and then climb the rest on foot (320 steps).

Taking the elevator costs a couple euros more but eliminates a couple hundred steps. This seems like a fair trade. Walking the entire way will save you money and instill a sense of accomplishment. But there's not much to see until you reach the interior balcony at the base of the dome which is where the lift stops.

From the balcony, climb the spiral staircase. The final section requires pulling yourself with a rope through a narrow opening. It requires some strength. And claustrophobes may need to take a few calming breaths. But once through, you're on top of St. Peter's with amazing views across Vatican City. The climb takes around 10 minutes.

## Post Office

Before descending to the bottom, exit at the rooftop terrace for more spectacular views. The terrace also has a water fountain, bathrooms, souvenir shop and a Vatican City post office box. Make use of the latter. Buy a postcard from the souvenir shop, fill it out and drop it in the yellow post box. Make sure you explain to the recipient how and where you sent the postcard.

There's still something special about sending and receiving postcards. Even in this era of Instagram and insta-everything, nothing beats sending a tangible, handwritten gift to friends and family. And a postcard is the cheapest and easiest way to do so. But why settle for a random sidewalk post box when you can send a postcard from the top of St. Peter's Basilica?

## How to Find It

St. Peter's anchors Vatican City in the eponymous Piazza San Pietro. You can't miss it. Get there on Metro line A at Ottaviano station. Or hop on tram #19 which stops at Risorgimento-San Pietro station. By bus, take #40 to Piazza Pia or #64, #62 and #81 to the Vatican. There's also a light rail stop at St. Pietro station which is most useful for those traveling from Rome's cruise port, Civitavecchia.

St. Peter's Basilica is open daily:

- April 1 to September 30: 7AM to 7PM
- October 1 to March 31: 7AM to 6PM

The dome is also open daily:

- April 1 to September 30: 8AM to 6PM
- October 1 to March 31: 8AM to 5PM

## Links

WEBSITE: vatican.va/various/basiliche/san_pietro/index_it.htm

GOOGLE MAP: goo.gl/maps/aeaUxxYsU5Uns9LZ9

# 23

# The Vatican Splurge

One of the most trafficked tourist destinations in Rome, attracting over 20,000 tourists a day in summer, budget money for a Vatican splurge. Instead of throwing elbows in the Sistine Chapel, throw money at the problem and you'll consider it the best splurge of your trip. That said, prepare yourself now—before you click those juicy tour links below—for the high price tag. As the old saying goes, "If you have to ask what it costs, then it's probably too much."

## Go Early

One way to see the Vatican without the crowds is to book a tour before it opens to the public.

With the Waking up the Vatican guided tour, you'll get a VIP tour before the doors open. The tour takes you through the Vatican with a small group, led by an official Vatican key-keeper who is turning on the lights with you. You'll see the Sistine Chapel, Raphael's Rooms and the Gallery of the Maps before the crowds come pouring in.

If you prefer a more private experience, you can book the Early Entry with Breakfast option. This tour starts with an American-style buffet breakfast at the Courtyard of the Pine Cone. Then, you will be free to tour the Vatican without a guide before it opens to the public.

## Go Late

Another way to avoid the crowds is to visit the Vatican after hours.

Vatican Night Tours allow you to visit the museums and Sistine Chapel after closing time with a small group, led by a guide. This tour also includes Raphael's Rooms, the Galleries of the Tapestries and the Candelabra and the Hall of Maps.

Alternatively, you can take advantage of the Vatican Night Openings. This allows you to visit with a group after closing time on select dates. This is a unique tour experience because, besides the tour of the museums and Sistine Chapel, they'll treat you to a concert!

## Go Rogue

There are other tour options that allow you to see things that aren't part of a typical tour.

For example, the Hidden Museums tour showcases sights such as the Niccoline Chapel and Bramante Staircase that are closed to the public. This is a guided tour, so you'll learn a lot about the Vatican while touring these restricted areas.

You could also book the Vatican Off-Limits tour. This tour is like the after-hours options, with one important addition: 30 minutes in the Sistine Chapel with just your tour group, and no one else. This is a great opportunity to view one of the world's foremost tourist destinations without the crowds.

## Links

WEBSITES:

- Waking up the Vatican: bit.ly/2XBkXU7
- Early Entry with Breakfast: bit.ly/2UBReZk
- Vatican Night Tours: bit.ly/2DwkgE3
- Vatican Night Openings: bit.ly/2IMY1gC
- Hidden Museums: bit.ly/2vky0NL
- Vatican Off-Limits: bit.ly/2DutC38

GOOGLE MAP: goo.gl/maps/BJXw5DTVVr75LHRX8

# 24

# As Michelangelo Intended

No matter where you go in Rome, you're close to a Michelangelo masterpiece. Sure the "Pietà" and "Moses" are stunning. But the Sistine Chapel ceiling remains Michelangelo's masterpiece.

Named after Pope Sixtus IV, the Sistine Chapel is now a part of the Vatican Museums. And it continues to serve as the pope's private chapel. Michelangelo was reluctant to accept the frescoes commission because he felt his best work came as a sculptor. Luckily for Western art, the Renaissance genius completed these Biblical frescoes between 1508-1512. Even today, the five million tourists who visit the Sistine Chapel annually stand in awe under Michelangelo's ceiling frescoes and before his 1541 altar fresco "The Last Judgment."

## Late Birds See the Finest Frescoes

Tourist crowds inundate the Sistine Chapel. In fact, once you get inside this chapel, it's often difficult to enjoy Michelangelo's masterwork. Why? Because thick crowds will make you feel like a sardine There is, however, an easy way you can enhance your Sistine Chapel experience. And you can do it for no extra fee.

Everyone says the "early bird catches the worm," right? But why not consider visiting the Sistine Chapel near closing time? One of the greatest benefits of visiting the Sistine Chapel late in the day is that you'll get to see the frescoes without artificial lighting. That's right, employees turn off the lights in the Sistine Chapel right before closing. The frescoes jump off the ceiling. They appear quasi-3d! You'll see the frescoes as Michelangelo intended. Relish these 10 minutes before museum staff kicks you out.

## How to Find It

The Sistine Chapel is in Vatican City on the western side of the Tiber River. It's open Monday through Saturday from 9AM to 6PM (ticket counter closes at 4PM) and on the last Sunday of every month from 9AM to 2PM (ticket counter closes at 12:30PM). Always reserve an entrance time in advance. Please note, the Sistine Chapel closes on many important Catholic holidays. Always check the calendar online before visiting. The closest Metro stop is Cipro-Musei Vaticani, a 10-minute walk away.

## Links

WEBSITE: museivaticani.va/content/museivaticani/en.html

GOOGLE MAP: goo.gl/maps/UQ4aSkdWv8zfsasx6

# 25

# Bernini's Forgotten Masterpiece

Some might consider it a shame that one of Earth's greatest chunks of marble sits in relative obscurity. Not me! I consider it an opportunity. Other than the occasional "Dan Brown" bus tour, few tourists visit Rome's Chiesa di Santa Maria della Vittoria. Here, in a quiet, locals-mostly church far from the selfie sticks, you'll find Bernini's stunning sculpture, "Ecstasy of Saint Teresa."

## A Brief History

After falling out with Pope Innocent X, sculptor Gian Lorenzo Bernini (1598-1680) needed a new patron. Then a cardinal named Federico Cornaro came calling. He wanted a sculpture for his family's chapel in Santa Maria della Vittoria Church. Cornaro asked Bernini to depict the spiritual visions of Spanish mystic Saint Teresa, who the church had canonized in 1622. Saint Teresa often wrote about visions of celestial beings, some of whom penetrated her heart with fiery arrows. Bernini depicted one such episode in his marble statue, "Ecstasy of

Saint Teresa," completed in 1652.

## Sexy or Sublime? Controversy Brews

The sculpture shocks many people who see "Ecstasy of Saint Teresa" for the first time because of just how erotic the work looks. St. Teresa appears to be moaning in mid-orgasm as a cherub gets ready to plunge his arrow into her heart. This explicit eroticism led one visiting Frenchman to quip, "Well, if that's divine love, I know all about it."

It's more likely, however, that Bernini was using sexual imagery as a motif to express spiritual ecstasy. The fresco above the central statue shows a dove, a symbol of the Holy Spirit. The natural light Bernini used suggests divine communion between St. Teresa and God. But the only way to decide what Bernini was up to is to go see it for yourself.

## Of Course, Dan Brown Wrote About It

The "Ecstasy of Saint Teresa" gained fame thanks to Dan Brown's best-seller "Angels & Demons." Despite the book's and movie's popularity, few tourists know where to find this masterpiece. Those intrepid travelers who make the journey receive a nearly private viewing as a reward.

## How to Find It

The church is on via Venti Settembre. It's a short walk from Termini Station or the Piazza della Repubblica Metro stop. To avoid those aforementioned Dan Brown tours, visit the Ecstasy of Saint Teresa in the early morning or late afternoon. The church opens for visitation on weekdays from 8:30AM to 12PM and 3:30PM to 6PM and between Mass services on Sunday.

Links

WEBSITE: chiesasantamariavittoriaroma.it

GOOGLE MAP: goo.gl/maps/CLdwFLXtnhDnpSdv5

# 26

# Keyhole with a View

L et's be frank: Though worth it, most of Rome's best-known tourist attractions are expensive and crowded. That's not the case with one special keyhole on Aventine Hill. Not only is it free, but it also affords an unforgettable view of St. Peter's Basilica in Vatican City. Every year, thousands of savvy tourists stand before the "Aventine Keyhole" for a keyhole-framed view of the most-famous dome in Christendom.

## Malta, Masons and Marvelous Gardens

What's commonly called the Aventine Keyhole is officially known as the Knights of Malta Keyhole. That's right, a famous Christian chivalric order runs this attraction on Piazza dei Cavalieri di Malta.

Most historians believe a rich guy named Alberico II owned a palace-like structure here dating back to the 930s. The Knights of Malta most likely took over ownership of this property in the 1400s. Famed architect Giovanni Battista Piranesi built the

Cavalieri di Malta, where the keyhole now stands, in the 1760s. Since the Knights of Malta own this keyhole, you'll be standing on the Republic of Malta's soil while in Italy! But, sorry, they won't stamp your passport.

Take a moment to admire the maritime-themed architecture. And keep your eyes peeled for Masonic symbols adorning the door. If you want to see what's behind the door and visit the Cavalieri di Malta's stunning gardens, schedule an appointment online.

### How to Find It

Find the Piazza dei Cavalieri di Malta at the intersection of via di S. Sabina and via di Porta Lavernale on Aventine Hill. The Circo Massimo is the closest Metro stop. Keep in mind it's only a 20-minute walk south from the Colosseum. So, it's an easy detour from central Rome's major ruins.

### Take Time to Smell the... Oranges

There's no need to rush away after you've peeped through the Aventine Keyhole. Unbeknownst to many tourists, there's a wonderful garden right around the corner. The Giardino degli Aranci ("Orange Garden") is so named for the pungent scent of its many orange trees. Whether the oranges are in season or not, you will enjoy an incredible 360-degree view of Rome.

## Links

WEBSITES:

- Knights of Malta: orderofmalta.int
- Orange Garden: bit.ly/2GEpIqo

GOOGLE MAPS:

- Knights of Malta Keyhole: goo.gl/maps/MdnQ92PfwC8xHacSA
- Orange Garden: goo.gl/maps/M2VzDbeFK1AGkFwD6

# 27

# A Pantheon Secret

I t's safe to say Rome's Pantheon has stood the test of time. Although the site's use for religious rites dates as far back as 750 BC, we can thank Emperor Hadrian for the Pantheon we see today. Consecrated around 126 AD, Hadrian built the Pantheon in homage to the many Roman gods. Pantheon translates to "all the gods." Thanks to bombproof construction and continual upkeep, the Pantheon remains one of the best-preserved ancient buildings in Rome.

## Get Ready for the Oculus

Circles (and squares) are all around, but the most-conspicuous circle is an opening in the center of the dome. This is called the oculus. This perfect circular opening lets in natural sunlight during the day and keeps the interior cool by letting hot air escape. It also serves as a handy sundial. And notice there's no glass covering the oculus. So it gets wet in here during a rain shower.

## View the "Florentine Find"

While everyone is gawking at the oculus, look for a lesser-known opening in the ceiling. This hole played a significant role in igniting the Renaissance. When you're inside the temple turn around and look above the main doors. Scan the lower third of the dome until you spot a tiny rectangular hole. Renaissance architect Filippo Brunelleschi cut this little hole to better understand the Pantheon's construction. At the time, Brunelleschi was working on the dome of Florence's Cathedral of Saint Mary of the Flower. All of Brunelleschi's studying paid off. In 1436, the Florentine "Duomo" overtook the Pantheon as the world's largest dome.

Today, neither holds the title for the largest dome in the world. However, the Duomo remains the world's largest masonry-built dome. Meanwhile, the Pantheon keeps the title for the largest unreinforced concrete dome.

## How to Find It

About halfway between Trevi Fountain and Campo de' Fiori, the Pantheon anchors the south end of Piazza della Rotonda. The Spanish Steps, Piazza Navona and Castel Sant'Angelo are a 15-minute walk away. By Metro, get off at Barberini station.

The Pantheon is open Monday through Saturday from 8:30AM to 7:30PM and on Sunday from 9AM to 6PM. Since there's no entry charge, prepare yourself to deal with hordes of tourists. Want a little more peace? Wake up early on a weekday and go inside right when it opens. You'll have about 10 minutes of relative solitude.

## Links

WEBSITE:
polomusealelazio.beniculturali.it/index.php?en/232/pantheon

GOOGLE MAP: goo.gl/maps/5Kxg5X4d1KU3HPgU8

# 28

# The Other Catacombs

Feeling drained from the Roman heat? No sweat! Time for a trip to northern Rome. Explore the "cool" (both literal and figurative) Catacombs of Priscilla. While not as popular as the Catacombs of San Sebastiano or San Callixtus, the Catacombs of Priscilla prove well worth your time. It's especially satisfying for ancient-art lovers. That many tourists don't know about these catacombs only means you'll enjoy a more intimate touring experience.

Above the Villa Ada park, this underground complex encompasses some 40,000 tombs running for 5 miles. All of it dug by hand from volcanic rock. With narrow passageways and a few small rooms called "*cubiculum*," the catacombs are revered for their early Christian frescoes.

## The Mysterious Priscilla

Although we don't know for certain, most historians believe Priscilla was the wife of a prominent Roman senator. Apparently, Priscilla donated this plot of land as a burial area for the

Christian community in the 2nd century. Because of the high number of popes and martyrs buried here, they sometimes refer to the Catacombs of Priscilla as the "Queen of the Catacombs." The two most-famous popes interred here are Pope Marcellinus and Pope Marcellus I.

But don't worry if you're squeamish. Grave-robbers removed all the bodies in these catacombs long ago.

## Don't Miss the Frescoes!

Keep your eyes peeled for Christian frescoes and symbols like the fish and anchor. Unfortunately, many guests miss the famous niche containing the world's first etching of the Madonna and Child. So ask where to look before descending into the catacombs.

One room of particular importance the Greek Chapel. Inside you'll find many colorful frescoes depicting scenes from both the Old and New Testaments.

One particular fresco depicts a veiled woman holding her hands to the sky. Some scholars believe this suggests early Christians allowed women to become priests. But others believe it's a symbolic representation of the woman's ascent into heaven. You can decide what interpretation you believe once you see this fresco for yourself.

## How to Find It

By Metro, get off at either the Libia or S. Agnese/Annibaliano stops. Both stations are a 20-minute walk away. The Borghese Gallery is only a 20-minute walk southeast of here. So it makes a logical adjacent attraction. Keep in mind the Borghese requires advanced reservations. The Catacombs of Priscilla are open from 9AM to 12PM and 2PM to 5PM every day except Monday. Because of ongoing restoration work, confirm opening hours on the website.

## Links

WEBSITE: catacombepriscilla.com/index_en.html

GOOGLE MAP: goo.gl/maps/bD1hH8MqFH5MwNUQ8

# 29

# Ruins Sans Ruinous Crowds

It's no secret the Ancient Romans loved a good bath. In fact, we wouldn't have spas today (at least, as we know them) had it not been for those hot-water-worshipping Romans. Many first-time tourists to Rome miss the ruins of one of the city's most opulent public baths: the Baths of Caracalla. However, travelers to Rome "in-the-know" (that's us!) consider its relative obscurity a selling point. Sparing a little extra time to visit the Baths of Caracalla rewards travelers with an intimate ruins experience. In the heart of Rome, no less.

## A Brief History

Although named for Emperor Caracalla, historians think his father, Emperor Septimius Severus, ordered construction in the early 200s AD. Completed in 216 AD, Romans considered them the most opulent baths in the city. Until they fell into disuse in the turbulent 6th century. The sacking of Rome sure didn't help.

Rome spared no expense building this luxurious complex. It contained vast indoor gathering spaces with marble floors, lush outdoor gardens and various heated and cooled rooms. Countless exquisite statues, mosaics and frescoes graced the interior. Several bathing areas, with multiple pools each, tied everything together. Historians believe over 1,500 Romans could frolic inside these baths at any one time.

Fun fact: The architects behind NYC's Pennsylvania Station and Chicago's Union Station drew inspiration from the Baths. Sadly, Penn Station lost this visual ode after a renovation in the 1960s.

## The Baths Today

The Baths of Caracalla make a nice detour from the main ruins district. Only about a mile from the Colosseum, head south on via di San Gregorio. Then turn left on Piazza di Porta Capena. Continue on viale della Terme di Caracalla. It's that easy. Get off at either Circo Massimo or Colosseo if riding the Metro.

The Baths of Caracalla are open from 9AM to 6:30PM Tuesday through Sunday and between 9AM to 2PM on Monday. Included on the recommended Roma Pass, the baths only cost about €6 per person. Spring for the audio guide so you can better appreciate these magnificent ruins.

Besides offering tours, the baths hold live music and theatrical performances in the summer. It's a good idea to check if any special events overlap with your visit.

## Links

WEBSITE: archeorm.arti.beniculturali.it/siti-archeologici/terme-caracalla (site down at publication time)

GOOGLE MAP: goo.gl/maps/BBTs9jYEVWAiBJuj8

# 30

# From Abattoir to Market

Once one of the busiest trading ports in the ancient world, the Testaccio district is south of old Rome along the Tiber River. And you can still find tangible evidence of those bustling times. The neighborhood's Monte Testaccio is a mountain made from ancient terracotta jars called amphorae.

Besides being a trading center, Testaccio was also home to Rome's slaughterhouses. After all those years of trade and slaughter, Testaccio developed a reputation for culinary excellence. Many foodies consider Testaccio to be the best place to get your grub on.

## Tasting Testaccio

Many of Rome's most-iconic dishes trace their origins to Testaccio. Just a few recipes credited to those industrious butchers include oxtail stew, Roman-style tripe and a good deal of offal-based dishes.

The best place to get a taste of the neighborhood is in the

bustling Testaccio Market. Here you'll find a dizzying array of fresh meats, seafood and produce for sale and dozens of fantastic food stalls. Just a few locals' favorite stalls include Le Mani in Pasta, Mordi e Vai and FoodBox. For a sit-down bite to eat, grab a slice of pizza at Pizzeria Da Remo or a pasta plate at award-winning Flavio al Velavevodetto.

## Three Exceptional Attractions

Although food is the top attraction here, a few noteworthy sights will keep you busy in between meals. The most-famous attraction is Monte Testaccio. As mentioned above, this is a mountain formed from amphorae terracotta pots. Long ago, these vessels stored essential foodstuffs during transport, including Italian staples like wine and olive oil. It's believed over 50 million discarded amphorae make up this famous hill.

Built from 18 to 12 BC, the Pyramid of Caius Cestius stands at a fork between two ancient roads and beside a modern Metro stop. Oh, the anachronism! This pyramid honors a dude named Caius Cestius, one of ancient Rome's leading magistrates and religious figures. Please note, you can only visit on the second and fourth Saturdays of every month and you have to schedule a visit beforehand.

Near the Pyramid of Cestius, the Protestant Cemetery attracts literature groupies. You'll discover the remains of not one but two of England's greatest Romantic poets: John Keats and Percy Bysshe Shelley. Other famous non-Catholics buried here include Goethe's son August von Goethe, Tolstoy's daughter Tatyana Tolstaya and Scottish artist Robert Michael Ballantyne.

## How to Find It

Reach Testaccio on the Metro at the Piramide station. Bus stops within walking distance include Ostiense/Piramide, Campo Boario and Campo Boario/Zabaglia. If you fancy a stroll, Testaccio is about a 30-minute walk south of the Jewish Ghetto.

## Links

WEBSITES:

- Testaccio Market: mercatoditestaccio.it
- Monte Testaccio: bit.ly/2IY9uKf
- Pyramid of Caius Cestius: bit.ly/2W3L6dL
- Protestant Cemetery: cemeteryrome.it/about/about.html

GOOGLE MAPS:

- Testaccio: goo.gl/maps/zbXBmjCCS782
- Testaccio Market: goo.gl/maps/Bou4rwPFkARmjPgv9
- Monte Testaccio: goo.gl/maps/eFwjbKYEZ900T2G19
- Pyramid of Caius Cestius: goo.gl/maps/V2BKxfLbAquzPB2x6
- Protestant Cemetery: goo.gl/maps/K3KRVCDXCkGcqZRu5

# 31

# Backdoor Neighborhoods

When you're feeling overwhelmed by central Rome's chaotic crowds, take a deep breath and cross over the Tiber River to Trastevere and Monteverde. In fact, consider basing yourself in one of these neighborhoods for a permanent refuge.

### Energetic & Historic

Located just south of the Vatican, Trastevere is a preserved medieval neighborhood. Complete with cobblestone streets, fascinating church-villas and packed with trendy restaurants and nightclubs, Trastevere warrants a half-day wander and a meal.

Named for its location to the west of the Tiber River, Trastevere has a history dating back to pre-Roman Etruscan times. As the Roman Empire grew, powerful citizens built extravagant villas here. None other than Julius Caesar built a villa on Gianicolo Hill.

Sadly, you can't visit Caesar's estate today. But you can visit some of the oldest churches in Rome. During the years when the empire outlawed Christianity, many wealthy Christians in Trastevere opened their villas to the faithful for Mass. A few of the oldest of these villas/churches now open to tourists include the Santa Cecilia ("Church of Santa Cecilia") and the Basilica di Santa Maria of ("Basilica of Our Lady in Trastevere"), the second of which is in the central piazza.

Nowadays, thanks to its multiple international university campuses, Trastevere attracts youthful and artsy residents. The global influence gives Trastevere an energetic and diverse vibe. You'll have no problem finding authentic food, craft beer and exciting nightlife opportunities. One suggestion is to do a food-themed walking tour.

## Above the Fray

Famous for sprawling Villa Doria Pamphilj Park, Monteverde lies just southeast of Trastevere. As you could tell from the name, Monteverde stands atop a hill overlooking Trastevere. Once you arrive in Monteverde, you'll leave the crowds far, far behind.

The main attraction in this quiet area is the massive Villa Doria Pamphilj, which is now Rome's largest public. Once a private residence, sunbathers, joggers and picnickers now rule this area. As do their four-legged friends.

Take a trip to Villa Sciarra, a fountain-filled park some historians believe Cleopatra visited. And stroll Monteverde's many artisan boutiques, *gelaterie* and restaurants before heading back to the heart of Rome.

## How to Find Them

From Termini, hop on bus N8 toward Gianicolense/casaletto and exit at the Trastevere/Min. Pubblica Instruzione stop. One of the closest bus stops to Monteverde's Villa Doria Pamphilj is Ozanam/Bottazzi, which can be reached on the N19 line.

## Links

GOOGLE MAPS:

- Trastevere: goo.gl/maps/mMnaqGwwAU52
- Monteverde: goo.gl/maps/eXmVHFfwFZAEK4te9
- Church of Santa Cecilia: goo.gl/maps/FH9sh1RBRH7iQS379
- Basilica Trastevere: goo.gl/maps/2b6Bz7ypiWP4Fzg57
- Villa Doria Pamphilj Park: goo.gl/maps/8coHhsHupz42
- Villa Sciarra: goo.gl/maps/pQN7tVFcvUHFtAYX6

# 32

# The Roman Ghetto

E veryone knows Rome is the epicenter of the Catholic faith. But did you know the Italian capital also claims Europe's oldest Jewish Ghetto? In 1555, Pope Paul IV forced Jews to live in this walled-in quarter because the area reeked of fish, flooded and was prone to disease. Nice guy, huh? It took over three centuries before city officials destroyed the Ghetto's walls. Ironically, the Roman-Jewish families who clung to their homes have had the last laugh; the Roman Ghetto contains the city's most-expensive real estate!

## The Ghetto Superstars

The Tempio Maggiore di Roma ("Great Synagogue of Rome") is the Roman Ghetto's must-see attraction. Established in 1904, it's one of the largest and most-significant Jewish temples in Italy. It's also home to a history museum on Roman Judaism. The Great Synagogue is open Sundays through Wednesdays between 10AM to 5PM and on Thursdays from 9AM to 5PM.

One of the most popular selfie-spots in the Roman Ghetto is

at the ancient sculpture, Bocca della Verità ("Mouth of Truth"). Weighing about one ton, this 1st-century marble mask most likely depicts a sea god. Look familiar? You might recall it from the Audrey Hepburn film "Roman Holiday." The reason it's called the "Mouth of Truth" is because of a rumor that the mask eats the hands of liars... So be careful!

But the main attraction here is walking. Wander the narrow cobblestone streets and let them take you back in time. Explore courtyards, tiny alleys and soak up this unique slice of Rome. Stop by the neighborhood's resident Roman ruin, the Teatro Marcello ("Theatre of Marcellus"). It's known playfully as the Jewish Colosseum. You'll see why.

## Eat Well... But Choose Wisely

Roman authorities locked shut the Jewish Quarter's walls every night. So, locals ate whatever they could find to stave off hunger. Many of the area's signature dishes harken to that era, with simple staples such as cod and artichokes. Of all the area's dishes, *carciofi alla giudìa* ("deep-fried artichoke") reigns supreme. And it's required eating to this day.

It's a sin to depart the Jewish Quarter hungry. But it's equally sinful to arrive at one of the neighborhood's historic restaurants without a reservation. Do yourself a favor and book a table 2-3 weeks in advance. Keep in mind that many restaurants take advantage of the area's culinary reputation to overcharge for mediocre fare. Do your research ahead of time. And don't make spontaneous, "hangry" dining decisions in this neighborhood.

## How to Find It

The Roman Ghetto lies on the Tiber River's eastern bank directly across from Isola Tiberna ("Tiber Island"). The streets via del Portico d'Ottavia, Lungotevere dei Cenci, via del Progresso and via di Santa Maria del Pianto roughly comprise its historical borders. Hop on bus #70 and exit at the Largo Torre Argentina. By Metro, exit at the Colosseo stop.

## Links

WEBSITES:

- Museo Ebraico: museoebraico.roma.it/en/the-museum
- Mouth of Truth: turismoroma.it/en/node/1513
- Teatro Marcello: turismoroma.it/en/teatro-marcello

GOOGLE MAPS:

- Synagogue & Museum: goo.gl/maps/j2qqSJATXcmrVBP7A
- Mouth of Truth: goo.gl/maps/hT1CEpd186sp28iy6
- Teatro Marcello: goo.gl/maps/Td8T7cXFQPuJyZzCA

# 33

# A Wee Village

About three miles south of the Colosseum, the Garbatella neighborhood is a hip oasis. It feels like a world apart from Rome. Garbatella garners comparisons to Paris' famed Montmartre district. Just like Montmartre, Garbatella has hopping performance venues, a vibrant arts scene and an eclectic mix of restaurants. And like Montmartre, it feels like its own village even though it's next to the city center. There is one notable exception though: Garbatella isn't as popular as Montmartre yet. So you won't encounter hordes of tourists. (At least for now...)

## Wee Britain in La Bella Roma

Italian urban planners designed Garbatella in a style influenced by Britain's garden city movement. During the 1920s, garden city adherents created livable, nature-filled neighborhoods for working-class people. You'll find wonderful interconnected community gardens and courtyards sprinkled throughout the Garbatella. Even the area's architecture, based on the ornamental Rococo style, boasts charming details from the natural world.

## Top Sights

As an up-and-coming center for the arts, Garbatella has some of Rome's most-dynamic street art and theaters. Marvelous street murals will stop you in your tracks. And the famous Teatro Palladium ("Palladium Theater") hosts film festivals, plays and live music events throughout the year. Although not as popular as the Palladium, the Teatro Ambra Garbatella ("Ambra Garbatella Theater") is another performing-arts venue worth checking out.

Garbatella is also part of the larger Ostiense quarter, home to several major attractions. In fact, this area hosts two top Christian sights: the Catacombs of Commodilla (containing one of the earliest images of a bearded Christ) and the Basilica of St. Paul. And the Centrale Montemartini museum, a renovated power plant, now displays ancient statues, mosaics and sarcophagi.

And if you came with an appetite, boy are you in luck. Rivaling perhaps only Trastevere in terms of foodie cachet, trendy and affordable eateries abound. With few tourist traps, you're almost guaranteed an honest meal here.

## How to Find It

Unsurprisingly, the closest metro stop to Garbatella is... Garbatella! A few local bus stops in the neighborhood include Carcereri, C.ne Ostiense/S. Galla, and Padre Giuliani.

## Links

WEBSITES:

- Palladium Theater: teatropalladium.uniroma3.it
- Ambra Garbatella Theater: teatroambra.it
- Basilica of St. Paul: basilicasanpaolo.org/index.asp?lang=eng
- Centrale Montemartini: centralemontemartini.org/en

GOOGLE MAP:

- Garbatella: goo.gl/maps/hiA57avZm3s
- Palladium Theater: goo.gl/maps/PmGRUWBRHzp8outp9
- Ambra Garbatella Theater: goo.gl/maps/Zkrv9iUuuG9jMiY18
- Basilica of St. Paul: goo.gl/maps/XoX4PDixCgW3MuiY6
- Centrale Montemartini: goo.gl/maps/LTDqeRpnfXw3n9zg9

# 34

# The Easy Day Trip

T he fascinating archeological site Ostia Antica is only 15 miles southwest of central Rome. Yet, most tourists don't even know it exists. At Ostia Antica, you won't have to deal with the hordes of tourists found at Pompeii and the Colosseum. Instead, you'll have space and solitude to appreciate a remarkably intact Roman city. Let Ostia whisk you back to a time of mule carts, togas, sandals and aqueducts.

## What's the Big Deal?

Archeologists believe humans have inhabited the area now called Ostia Antica since at least the 3rd century BC. It wasn't until Romans arrived in 400 BC, however, that this port city gained some serious power. In fact, historians believe this was Rome's first conquest, albeit a peaceful one. In effect, it birthed the Roman Empire.

Thanks to its ideal location at the "mouth" of the Tiber River ("ostium" roughly translates to "mouth"), Ostia Antica became a prosperous trading city and a significant naval base for the upstart city-state that'd one day grow to become the vaunted Roman Empire.

When the Roman Empire fell, Ostia Antica came tumbling down with it. The port silted up and the world lost Ostia under thick layers of mud, preserving it for centuries. Interestingly, Benito Mussolini was the first to order successful excavations at Ostia Antica.

Modern visitors experience a visceral sense of how people lived in this prosperous port town. Tour the many intriguing buildings, marvel over the exquisite frescoes. A few highlights include the forum shopping area, the temples for followers of Mithraism and arguably Europe's oldest synagogue.

Grab the audio guide for an extra €5. While bland, it'll help you appreciate and comprehend Ostia Antica's labyrinth of ruins.

## How to Find It

To get to Ostia Antica using public transport, first ride Metro line B to the Piramide stop. Once you get to the station, look for "Lido" signs and follow them to the Roma Porta San Paolo train station. Trains depart for Lido every 15 minutes and you can use a Metro ticket to get on. The ride from this station to Ostia Antica is about 30 minutes. Upon arrival, walk over the sky bridge and down Via della Stazione di Ostia Antica to the park entrance.

Ostia Antica opens every day from 8:30AM to 7:15PM in summer. In winter, it closes as early as 4:30PM. Always check the website in advance for current pricing and closures and schedule changes.

## Quick Tip: Bring a Picnic

I recommend packing a picnic lunch. As of today, there aren't many dining options in this area. But save your appetite for dinner. On your return trip to Rome, exit at the Piramide Metro stop and dine in the Testaccio neighborhood, home to one of the city's best restaurant scenes.

## Links

WEBSITE: ostiaantica.beniculturali.it

GOOGLE MAP: goo.gl/maps/negWkkjz98awoCTY8

# 35

# The Hard Day Trip

With 2.5 million visitors every year, the Pompeii archeological site is one of Italy's top tourist draws. And good news travelers: It's possible to reach Pompeii on a day trip from Rome.

Fair warning, though: A quick trip this is not. (Thanks Yoda!) You will spend about four hours traveling by train round-trip. Also, prepare yourself to deal with crowds of tourists clogging Pompeii's every nook and cranny. Acknowledging these inevitable inconveniences beforehand will cause a more satisfying experience should you take the Pompeii-in-a-day plunge.

You: This "Pompeii" Sounds Intriguing. Tell Me More

Me: Ok!

Located 15 miles south of Naples, Pompeii was a wealthy city at the height of the Roman Empire. On August 24, 79 AD that all ended. Nearby Mount Vesuvius erupted, killing at least 20,000 people and devastating both Pompeii and its neighbor Herculaneum. Since volcanic ash covered Pompeii and Herculaneum for centuries, experts consider them Italy's best-preserved ancient cities. In fact, archeologists continue to discover frescoes, household objects and bodies of victims. Taken together, they help tell the story of this once-prosperous town.

## How to Reach Pompeii From Rome

First off, it's way cheaper and more convenient to transfer in Naples rather than buying a one-way ticket from Rome to Pompeii. Pre-book a Super Economy one-way ticket from Rome to Naples on the Frecciarossa (FR) high-speed train. This trip takes about 70 minutes. Once you arrive at Naples Centrale Station, head downstairs toward the Circumvesuviana Railway station. On the Circumvesuviana line, you can catch a train to Pompeii Scavi–Villa Dei Misteri. These trains depart every 30 minutes. So no need to book ahead. The trip from Naples to Pompeii takes about 35 minutes.

To get home, reverse your route on the Circumvesuviana back to Naples. Then buy a ticket to Rome from one of the many self-service ticket machines in Naples Centrale. By purchasing one-way tickets, you won't have to worry about rushing through the ruins of Pompeii. Instead, you can return to Rome at your leisure.

## Ticketing Tips

Pompeii's open every day:

- 8:30AM–5PM from November till March
- 8:30AM–7:30PM from April till October

Usually, you'll find a long line of people waiting in front of the Porta Marina entrance. If this is the case when you visit, then walk three minutes to the lesser-known ticket booth near Hotel Vittoria. Once you have your tickets in hand, return to Porta Marina. Before entering, however, be sure to grab a complimentary guidebook and map to help you better understand the layout of the city.

## Don't Forget Herculaneum!

While you're in the area, why not squeeze in a tour of the nearby ruins at Herculaneum? You've come all this way. Believe it or not, many archeologists think Herculaneum's ruins are more impressive than Pompeii's. So, not only will you get to see incredible baths, frescoes and temples, you won't have to contend with the hordes of tourists like at Pompeii. To reach Herculaneum, exit at the Ecolano station, which is on the Circumvesuviana line about halfway between Naples and Pompeii. Herculaneum has the same opening and closing hours as Pompeii.

## Links

WEBSITE: pompeiisites.org/en

GOOGLE MAPS:

- Pompeii: goo.gl/maps/DDLP3EFhQCJ7CLkb9
- Herculaneum: goo.gl/maps/VWRtHiLM3XcjutP49

# III

# Indulge

*Dining Tips – Food Culture – Famous Dishes –
Restaurants*

# 36

# The Italian Meal, Explained

Roman meals are lengthy social events. While Roman cooking came from the *"cucina povera"*—home cooking of the commoner—a meal's structure is anything but simple. In fact, Romans follow a formal procession. It's so ingrained, many follow it without even trying. It's just the natural way of doing things come meal time.

So what makes up an "Italian meal?" I've described the courses in order below. Not all meals include every course. At restaurants, you can pick-and-choose which courses you want. But a formal, exhaustive dinner includes most if not all the following courses.

## Aperitivo

Similar to an appetizer, the *aperitivo* opens a meal. Most Romans take an *aperitivo* while standing with a wine, *prosecco* or spritz. Occasionally, they eat tiny foods, such as olives, chips, nuts or cheese.

## Antipasto

The *antipasto* is a heavier starter. Served cold, popular options include charcuterie (salami, mortadella, prosciutto, etc.), cheese, little sandwiches (*panino*, *bruschetta*, *crostino*), fresh vegetables and fish or shrimp.

## Primo

The first course is called the *primo*. It comprises hot food and is heavier than the *antipasto*. But it remains lighter than the second course. Meatless dishes form the heart of any "*primo piatto*." Examples include risotto, pasta, soup and broth, gnocchi, polenta and lasagne.

## Secondo e Contorno

Typically, the *secondo* means meat and fish. Expect turkey, sausage, pork, beef, cod, stockfish, salmon, lobster, lamb or chicken. Meats are grilled or stewed. You'll find a variety of grilled vegetables ("*contorno*") served alongside the *secondo*.

## Insalata

If the *contorno* had many leafy vegetables, they might omit the salad. Otherwise, a simple garden salad arrives at this point.

## Formaggi e Frutta

Italians dedicate an entire course to local cheese and fresh seasonal fruit. Just when you think you can't eat anymore, find space for this treat. Not only will your tastebuds thank you, but so will your digestive tract.

## Dolce

After cheese and fruit, the *dolce*, or dessert, arrives. The options are endless. But popular desserts include tiramisu, *panna cotta*, chocolate cake and pie. At Christmastime, you'll also see *panettone* and *pandoro* on menus. You can always enjoy an ice-cold gelato or *sorbetto* for dessert, too.

## Digestivo con Caffè

The *digestivo*, also called *ammazza-caffè* if served after the coffee, is the drink to conclude the meal. Order a light spirit, such as grappa, amaro or limoncello. Coffee is often drunk last, even after the *digestivo*. Italians do not have milky coffees or drinks after meals. Instead, they favor strong coffee such as an espresso.

# 37

# Eateries Definition Guide

Do you know the difference between a trattoria and osteria? How about a taverna and bar? You should: It all comes down to expectations. (But, then again, isn't everything in life?)

Once "hangry" time sets in after sightseeing for hours, knowing the difference between Rome's various eateries and how they differ from their North American counterparts can make or break your meal. For example, it's perfectly wise to belly up to a bar for breakfast. Gasp! And that's only the tip of the gastronomic iceberg. Read below for a rundown on all the main eateries in Rome and what you can expect at each. Note: I ordered this list from most expensive and most formal to most affordable and most casual. Roughly.

**Ristorante** (ree-stoh-RAHN-teh): Full table service. Price, service and quality levels vary within the "*ristorante*" label. But they are Italy's most expensive and formal dining option. The distinction between a *ristorante* and *trattoria* gets blurry nowadays. Expect long menus, big portions, impeccable service and 3+ courses. Dress for a formal but not stifling atmosphere. Extensive wine list. Reservations recommended.

**Trattoria** (trah-toh-REE-ah): Full table service. Cheaper, smaller and more casual than a *ristorante*. Often the biggest difference "resides" in location—restaurants occupy glitzy spaces on main thoroughfares. Trattorie sit on quieter, low-rent side streets. Trattoria quality, however, can meet or exceed a ristorante but come at a fraction of the price. "Trats" are frequently family run with a husband-and-wife duo cooking and running the show. Solid wine list. Reservations recommended.

**Osteria** (aw-steh-REE-ah): Full table service. Cheaper, smaller and more casual than a trattoria. Many *osterie* are beloved neighborhood landmarks, serving the after-work and family crowd. You'll find some of the best eating in central Rome at out-of-the-way little osterie at which no one beyond a 10-block radius travels to eat. Frequently family run. Often have a cozy bar. Solid wine list. Reservations recommended.

**Bar** (bahrrr): Bar and self-service. More like what we would consider a neighborhood cafe, a true community hive. Open all day serving light meals, coffee and alcohol. Limited menu: Pastries for breakfast (properly taken while standing at the bar). Tramezzino (triangular) and demi-baguette sandwiches for lunch. At most, a couple pastas and a meat dish for dinner. Often eat standing up at the bar or at a few small tables. Solid wine list.

**Enoteca** (eee-no-tech-AH): Bar and self-service. Wine bar specializing in regional wines. Serving finger foods and small bites from a buffet on or beside the bar. Extensive wine list.

**"-eria"**: Table, counter and self-service. Add this suffix to the end of a food name and that means a place specializing in that food. Examples include the pizzeria (pizza, duh), *bruschetteria* (bruschetta), *spaghetteria* (spaghetti, double-duh) and the all-important *gelateria* (GELATO!!!). Now, this doesn't mean they only serve that one food. But they limit other selections. And, frankly, you go to an "-eria" to eat the namesake food. Limited wine list.

**Taverna** (tah-VEHR-nah): Bar and self-service. Small rustic eatery based around the bar with a limited menu, serving lunch and dinner. Neighborhood-driven and the focus on food versus drinks varies (usually: drinks). Expect a small menu serving a couple pastas and a couple meats. Consider tavernas the dinner counterpart to breakfast and lunch-focused bars. Solid wine list.

**Rosticceria** (roh-stee-cheh-REE-ah): Counter service. Notable as an "-eria" that doesn't specialize in a particular food, but a cooking method—slow-roasting meats. A *rosticceria* specializes in spit-roasted chicken and other meats. You'll often find pre-made meals besides whatever is being roasted. Served primarily to-go. Might have a standup bar or a few tables. Great for takeout dinner but also serving lunch.

**Tavola Calda** (TAH-voh-lah KAHL-dah): Counter service. "Hot tables" are Italy's version of fast food. Order pre-made dishes by the plate or weight to-go or eat standing up at a bar to the side of the buffet. See your food before you order it. Serving lunch and dinner. Cheap, filling and fast, there's no shame in refueling at a *tavola calda* on occasion.

**Pizza a Taglio/Pizza Rustica**: Counter service. To-go pizza joints pushing slices, sodas and beers. Sometimes a couple pasta dishes and desserts. Expect nowhere to eat, sitting or standing. In fact, many places are simple sidewalk counters. Awesome for a grab-and-go snack while sightseeing.

# 38

# Do You Have a Reservation? Part 2

his chapter demands no cheeky opener. No filler required. Instead, let me make it crystal clear at the outset: Rome is a bustling city where tables at great restaurants go fast. Therefore, make reservations for most of your lunches and all of your dinners.

Sure, you can wing it. But don't expect a table at Rome's popular restaurants for either meal. Wherever you have your heart set on eating, reserve a table by calling, emailing, going online or in-person at least a few days in advance. Make the reservation even earlier if it's for Friday or Saturday dinner. For famous restaurants and travel during peak summer season, extend the reservation timeline to two or three weeks out. More than a month might be overkill. Then again...

## Doing the Math

Why is making restaurant reservations so important? After all, Rome has like a billion eateries, right? To answer that, let's do the "math." (Side note: With no numbers, this is my kind of math!)

1. **The idea that "no matter where you eat in Rome, you'll eat well" is a myth.** While it might have been true once upon a time, terrible tourist traps now saturate Rome. These restaurants cater only to tourists. They serve Italian-American food. They don't care about developing loyalty through quality since tourists don't return. A lot of Rome's restaurants just aren't worth it.

   The math so far: Rome has fewer "great" restaurants left.

2. **Great restaurants only offer one or two seatings per meal.** Consider dinner: It starts between 8PM and 9PM and kitchens shut down around 11PM. (This isn't Spain.) So you've got a small reservation window of three hours. And Romans linger over dinner for at least 90 minutes.

   The math so far: Fewer "great" restaurants left + one or two seatings per meal.

3. **Restaurants are small.** Remember: Rome is over 2,000 years old. Have you ever considered how much time and money it takes to renovate a 2,000-year-old building? So Rome's restaurants make do with the space they have, which sometimes means a couple dozen tables.

   The math so far: Fewer "great" restaurants left + one or two seatings per meal + minimal tables available.

4. **Competition among hungry travelers is fierce.** Some 10 million people visit Rome every year. Plus, you know, people live here. And everybody's got to eat.

   The math so far: Fewer "great" restaurants left + one or two seatings per meal + minimal tables available + millions of people.

In sum: Fewer "great" restaurants left + one or two seatings per meal + minimal tables available + millions of people = **MAKE RESERVATIONS**.

# 39

# The Value Menu

No, you won't find a dollar menu in any self-respecting Roman restaurant. And you sure as hell won't find any five-dollar foot-longs. (Plus, "five euro 30-centimeters" just doesn't have the same ring to it.) But fear not fellow bargain hunters because Rome offers an altogether different type of value menu: The *menu turistico* and *menu del giorno.*

The set-price *menu turistico* ("tourist menu") and *menu del giorno* ("menu of the day") typically includes:

- A three- or four-course meal: A pre-defined combination of starters, pastas, meats and fish, side dishes and desserts.
- House wine: A half-quart carafe of your choice, white or red.

Many of these set-price menus represent solid bargains. Not only are they cheaper than buying each course a la carte, but they're often exempt from cover and table-service charges.

When faced with the choice opt for the *menu del giorno.* It's often of higher quality than a *menu turistico* and rotates more frequently. So, it's fresh and seasonal. The tourist menu, on the other hand, rarely changes. And since it's aimed at satisfying travelers' preconceived notions of Roman cuisine, the offerings are often bland and banal. That said, consider them both when choosing restaurants. Pick the one that fits your budget and tastebuds.

# 40

# Let's Get Tipsy

A mericans are used to tipping everywhere they go. Italians? Not so much. Therefore, on your grand tour of Rome, never feel obligated to leave a tip for anyone. Period. This is true in the restaurants, bars and cafes. In fact, the eatery probably already factored a tip into your bill. So don't sweat it!

This doesn't mean you can't leave a few euros for a waiter who provided exceptional service. A good standard for restaurant tipping is to leave about €1-2 per person for five-star service. Alternatively, you could just round up your bill to show your appreciation to the restaurant staff. Any tip over 10 percent, however, is far too high by Italian standards.

## Pricey Pane & Sneaky Servizio

When you receive your restaurant bill, look out for these two words: "*pane*" and "*servizio.*" Unlike America's beloved Olive Garden, bread bowls in Italy aren't free. Don't go into shock when you see the Italian word for "bread" ("*pane*") listed on your bill with a small fee. Typically, you'll see only €2 by the *pane* line. If you don't want to pay this hidden fee, tell your waiter you don't want bread at the start of your meal.

The other additional fee you might see listed on a restaurant receipt is for "service" (*servizio*). This extra fee should only appear on your bill if you're dining with a large party. Good restaurants should only list the *servizio* fee if your group is over eight people. Basically, the service charge functions as a tip for your waiter. Don't bother leaving a tip if your bill has this fee listed.

## Taxis, Porters & Guides... Oh My!

Besides waiters, you might be tempted to tip taxi drivers, hotel porters and tour guides. While tips are not obligatory in any of these cases, it has become increasingly common for tourists to tip the latter two professions.

Just like with restaurant waiters, your taxi fare already includes a tip. You could round up your final price to thank your taxi driver, but it's never necessary.

However, with hotel porters and concierges, it's a good idea to tip for great service. This is especially the case if your sweaty porter just schlepped heavy luggage up to your room. Again, there's no standard tip for porters, but a €5 note is a nice gesture.

Last, if you feel your guide really helped you get the most out of the Eternal City, give him/her a tip. Just don't go crazy. Tip a private tour guide 10 euros/person and a group tour guide 2-3 euros/person. You shouldn't feel the need to tip a tour guide over 10% of what you paid for the tour.

# 41

## The Coperto Caution

There you are waltzing Rome's cobblestone streets, hankering for a caffeine break, when you spot a sandwich board advertising €1 coffees. Done! You grab a table and sip a rich, steamy espresso. It tastes great. The caffeine rush is better. Ready to continue sightseeing, you drop a euro coin on the table before noticing the bill says €3. *What?!* But the sign says €1 coffees! It's a scam!

Well, no. It's not a scam. Instead, you've been up-charged. Discreetly up-charged with a "*coperto*," the table-service fee or cover charge. That €1 coffee you saw advertised? That's the standing-at-the-bar cost. The price jumps when you sit at a table. While lounging with your drink is relaxing, it can cost you more money in Italy's popular tourist cities, like Rome (and Venice, Florence, etc).

## One Cafe. Two Prices.

Specifically, establishments with a standing bar-top like bars, ice cream parlors, pizzerias and cafes have two menu prices. One for patrons who order and stand at the bar. And one for those who sit at a table. Therefore, it may be cheaper if you opt to stand while eating or drinking.

Sometimes, the price for sitting is double or even triple the price for standing. Why? Customers are more likely to finish their food or drinks quickly if they're standing. So the cheaper price encourages quick turnover. Furthermore, servers don't expect tips in Rome. So the extra money you pay for sitting helps cover the wages of the additional work of the servers.

Now, not all establishments have this pricing scheme. Restaurants, where everyone expects to sit back and enjoy a leisurely meal, typically only have a single price list. The bar is the indicator. If the place has a standing bar, then expect it to offer two prices for drinks and food.

## Stand or Sit?

There are several things to consider before you decide whether to sit or stand while grabbing a drink or some ice cream. First, look at the prices on the menu and see just how big of a difference there is. Even if you're hoping to sit at a table, you may change your mind once you see how many euros you could save by standing at the bar. In addition, consider your own personal needs. If you've spent a long day sightseeing around the city and your feet are killing you, paying a little more for a table and chair may be worthwhile.

Finally, don't forget to factor in the setting. Locals, who get to enjoy the city every day, opt to stand for the cheaper price. For them, the ideal situation is to order, toss back their drink and be on their way in a few minutes. However, you're in the city to sightsee. And if the cafe or bar has outdoor seating that allows you to enjoy a beautiful piazza with monuments, fountains and people-watching, seize the opportunity to have a leisurely drink at a cozy table. View the extra few euros as an admission price.

# 42

# Bet on the House

When ordering wine in Rome, seek a quality house wine. House wine (Italian: vino della casa) refers to bulk wine served at restaurants. You'll find it costs much less than its bottled-and-labeled brethren. Speaking of which, house wine arrives by the glass or carafe. Rarely will you find it bottled.

So, what is house wine exactly? That's the thing. There's no set definition for it. In fact, it's always fun discovering what kind of house wine is on offer at each restaurant. Originally, restaurants produced their own house wines. But that's exceedingly rare nowadays. Sometimes restaurants use their house wine to highlight local specialties. Some restauranteurs strike a deal directly with a winemaker for barrels of excellent wine, sparing the winemaker from bottling, labeling and wholesale-selling. Still other times, sadly, house wines are an excuse to get rid of an over-supply of vino.

## Is House Wine Worth It?

For many people, "house wine" is synonymous with low-to-middling quality. Honestly, this isn't always the case at all. Especially in a city like Rome, with such a long history of exceptional winemaking, it's easy to find a surprisingly good house wine.

At roughly half the cost of a bottle, ordering house wine will save a ton of money over the duration of your trip. While still enjoying one of Italy's favorite pastimes: drinking great wine with family and friends. Although, not all house wines are "diamonds in the rough," restaurants with a good reputation and authentic family run joints take pride in offering quality house wine.

## How to Order It

For those who want to flex their language muscles, memorize these phrases:

- "*Prendiamo un quarto di rosso della casa.*"
- "*Prendiamo un mezzo litro di rosso della casa.*"

The first sentence roughly translates to, "bring us a quart of the red house wine." In the second sentence, the speaker is asking for a "half liter" rather than a "quart." If you're more in the mood for a white house wine, then substitute the "*rosso*" with "*bianco.*"

## Tips for Finding Fantastic House Wine

Before committing to the house wine, ask your waiter for a taste using the following:

- *"Posso assaggiare il vino della casa?"*

Ask your waiter questions like what kinds of house wine they offer and what region(s) they come from. The more detailed responses you receive, the more likely this house wine is legit.

Also, don't expect high-quality house wines in places that don't have decent wine lists and food menus to begin with. While the occasional hole-in-the-wall dive pours a phenomenal house wine, the odds of this happening grow slim in tourist-centric Rome. Your best bet for landing a tasty house wine is at established and/or family run restaurants, ones frequented by locals. You know, like the ones recommended later in this chapter.

# 43

# Veggies to the Side

At first glance, Rome's cuisine looks like all meat and carbs. And to a certain extent, it is. However, restaurants in Rome also serve an array of hearty vegetable dishes. In fact, travelers who don't eat meat or just want a light meal will find plenty of vegetarian options. Chefs here specialize in braised, grilled and sautéed veggies. But you have to know where to look.

## How to Find Veggies

Once you get a menu in your hands, flip to the "*contorni*" section. Here, in the side dishes, you'll find a delicious assortment of cooked and raw veggies. Assemble a healthy meal by ordering three or more of these smaller plates. Remember to remind your waiter to bring them out together with the main meal.

Just be careful there aren't "hidden" meats in your veggie dish. For instance, many soups have a base of chicken or beef broth and chefs often use pork with cooked vegetables. If you have questions, ask your waiter "*E senza carne?*" ("There's no meat, right?").

## Popular Veggie Dishes

Rome is the epicenter of artichoke awesomeness. During peak season in April, you'll find this superfood in loads of recipes including soups, pies and pastas. First, try them Roman-style, "*carciofi alla Romana.*" This beloved braised dish incorporates fresh herbs like parsley and mint. They burst with distinctive Italian flavors like garlic, white wine and lemon.

Next, hunt down some Jewish-style artichokes. Another delicious way to sate your artichoke fix, deep-fried "*carciofi alla guida*" hail from Rome's historic Jewish Ghetto. These crispy snacks come with a refreshing spritz of lemon.

Come autumn, be on the lookout for pumpkin specialties like pumpkin carpaccio, pumpkin risotto and pumpkin ravioli, "*tortelli di zucca.*"

Another famous veggie is "*broccoletti,*" found on menus between autumn and spring. English speakers know it as "broccoli rabe (raab)." Usually Roman chefs cook it in salted water and transfer it to a pan with olive oil, sautéed garlic and red pepper flakes. You might also find *broccoletti* mixed in with various pasta dishes.

## Beware of Salads

Exotic salads and salads-as-meals haven't caught on in Rome. Unless you're talking about a few crafty, profit-driven restaurateurs. If you're in a Roman restaurant and see an extensive salad selection, then you're most likely in a tourist trap. Authentic Italian restaurants offer one or two simple green side salads.

That's it. Nothing more. But remember: Jump to the *contorni* section for your veggie fix.

# 44

# A Shepherd's Meal Endures

Of all the classic Roman dishes, none commands the loyalty of good old *cacio e pepe*. "Cheese and pepper" reigns supreme as Rome's undisputed king of comfort food. For thousands of years, Romans have sustained themselves on this simple, yet oh-so-satisfying, cheesy pasta dish.

Most historians believe *cacio e pepe* originated in the Apennine Mountains. Hardworking shepherds needed easy-to-make meals. They also had to use ingredients that wouldn't spoil quickly. Dried pasta, *pecorino romano* and black pepper fit the bill. And, yes, traditional *cacio e pepe* uses only three ingredients: *tonnarelli* pasta, *pecorino romano* cheese and freshly ground pepper. No butter. No oil. It doesn't even require other cheeses or spices.

Today, *cacio e pepe* remains Rome's most-iconic pasta dish. Thus, most restaurants in Rome serve this staple, delighting both locals and travelers.

## How to Make Authentic Cacio e Pepe

Even if your cooking expertise ends at pouring cereal into a bowl, you can master *cacio e pepe*. First, resist the temptation to add a lot of enhancements. Authentic *cacio e pepe* demands restraint. You need only water, salt, pepper, *tonnarelli* pasta and *pecorino romano* cheese.

First, boil salted water and add *tonnarelli* pasta, cooking until it's just barely al dente. Before pouring the pasta into a colander, reserve a few cups of pasta water. Next, pour about one cup of reserved pasta water into another pot and add pepper. Bring this mixture to a boil and then put in the pasta, adding more pasta water if needed. Add in grated *pecorino romano* and stir until it reaches a creamy consistency. Last, put the pasta into a serving bowl and add more pepper or grated cheese if desired.

## Why Tonnarelli?

The foodies out there have, by now, no doubt noticed that the traditional pasta used in making *cacio e pepe* is *tonnarelli* not spaghetti. Most *cacio e pepe* recipes you'll find use spaghetti because it's more readily available. Many chefs, however, consider the taste of traditional *tonnarelli* (which is like a thicker, eggier spaghetti) better complements the cheese sauce. You could substitute whatever pasta you prefer, but authentic *cacio e pepe* uses *tonnarelli*. Done. Full stop.

# 45

# Picnicking Like a Pro

L et's get this out of the way first: Rome officially discourages people from eating and drinking at historic monuments in the old center. Respectful travelers understand why: Trash gets left behind. Groups of picnickers block important access points. Overall, it detracts from the experience of seeing Rome's great monuments in the flesh. Er, the stone.

Technically, police can fine violators. Although, that rarely happens. That said, Italy's tourist cities have been clamping down on eating and drinking around, in and on historic monuments with increasing frequency. It's a noble effort. And it seems to gain momentum with every tourist season. So, by the time you're reading this, the rules may have changed. Rome may enforce their bans or enacting stricter ones.

To picnic like a pro, keep abreast of rule changes. I sure do. In the meantime, here are some helpful guidelines and locations for your picnicking adventures.

## Picnicking Dos

- **Snack on church steps.** Church steps are like neutral territory. While you don't want to block anyone's access or linger too long, it's okay to enjoy quick snacks, sandwiches and sodas on church steps. Except at St. Peter's.
- **Lay down a blanket in a park.** Rome's parks allow picnicking. Find a bench or a grassy spot, then feast and relax.
- **Carry a refillable water bottle.** Free water fountains abound in Rome and single-use plastic is travel's dirty secret. Plus, Rome struggles with its trash collection. Something you may notice on your trip. Save money and landfill space by using a refillable water bottle.
- **Picnic discreetly around major sights.** As stated above, authorities do not allow this. However, frequently I've munched on a panino and sipped a beer inside or around major attractions. But understand that the more famous the monument, the less likely you'll get away with picnicking. Pro tip: Keep your food and drink in your backpack on your lap, only removing it to nibble and sip.
- **Hit the markets.** Nothing brings a traveler closer to locals than shopping at an open-air market. Try out your survival Italian. Ask questions about where the food comes from, what it tastes like. Heck, request a sample. Pro tip: For the best selection, arrive early.
- **Grab a panino sandwich, roasted chicken or pizza to-go.** Not every picnic requires a blanket, wine and a cheese course. Quick-and-easy, pre-made picnics count, too!
- **Have your wine uncorked at the shop.** Unless you're carrying a corkscrew, you don't want to try fishing out the cork using a plastic fork. Trust me. Anywhere that sells

wine will have a corkscrew at the register counter.

## Picnicking Don'ts

- **Eat or drink on shop windowsills and steps.** They're trying to make a living and that wonderfully curated shop window isn't a seat. It's a consumer magnet.
- **Picnic around St. Peter's in Vatican City.** Unlike the rest of Rome, Vatican City enforces their no eating-and-drinking policy, especially in St. Peter's Square.
- **Get intoxicated.** Keep the wine and beer consumption in check during daytime hours.
- **Leave trash behind.** Find a trash can. And no matter how full it already is, use it.

## Almost Secret Spots

- Borghese Gardens: goo.gl/maps/QuyqA17ewoquQ1qx9
- Capo di Bove: goo.gl/maps/JwW8j8RVFJ9L2Med8
- Giardino degli Aranci: goo.gl/maps/Eoq2GEQAD1j9j5pR7
- Forum Boarium: goo.gl/maps/yLWmHB2bRMfamPKU6
- Parco del Celio: goo.gl/maps/MYHo6GoSm7kLWpaE9
- Hippodrome of Domitian: goo.gl/maps/sMpcAy7obW2BquVy9
- Aqueduct Park: goo.gl/maps/vMbHRd3yuf8ykw3c9
- Isola Tiberina: goo.gl/maps/SoUopSoEcy55Zs9g6

# 46

# Panini Perfection

S troll through Rome's Testaccio Market and you're bound to come across a long line in front of stall #15. What's the big fuss? Everyone's queueing for renowned sandwich-maker, Mordi e Vai.

Although it has only been around for less than a decade, Mordi e Vai has become Rome's go-to joint for a quick panino fix. In fact, this humble lunch counter has attained cult-like status amongst foodies. It's earning accolades from professional food critics and high praise from diners on Yelp, TripAdvisor, etc.

Local butcher Sergio Esposito and his wife opened this humble food stall in 2012. They felt Rome lacked a high-quality and affordable Roman-style panini customers could eat on-the-go. Hence the name Mordi e Vai, which is slang Italian for "Bite and Go." And how can you argue with a deli that touts its product as, "The super very best sandwich in Rome"? The fact is, you can't.

## Peasant's Price Point

You'll be hard-pressed to find a food stall more Roman than Mordi e Vai. The recipes here are so old you won't even find them at most sit-down restaurants. Esposito is a culinary preservationist, keeping Rome's culinary traditions alive. And he does it while keeping prices affordable.

If you're unsure what to order, opt for the most-popular panino: *allesso di scottona con cicoria*. "*Scottona*" refers to a tender heifer (young, childless female cow) meat often used in Roman cuisine. Esposito places this slow-cooked beef on crispy ciabatta bread along with a chicory sprig for added flavor. Once you take a bite of this savory sandwich, you'll know why the *allesso di scottona* is Mordi e Vai's top seller.

Mordi e Vai also serves a wide variety of panini with tripe (stomach lining). The most traditional of these panini is the *trippa alla Romana*, which includes a hearty tomato sauce, pecorino cheese and sprigs of mint. If tripe isn't your thing, then consider another Roman staple: the braised oxtail sandwich.

Not ready to give these traditional Roman delicacies a try? No worries! Mordi e Vai cooks up a mean meatball sandwich smothered in tomato sauce and juicy veal dipped in wine. For you vegetarians out there (bless you, child), Mordi e Vai also makes an awesome artichoke-and-cheese panino.

## How to Find It

Mordi e Vai's official address is Nuovo Mercato Comunale di Testaccio, Via Beniamino Franklin, 12/E. But the better address is Testaccio Market, box #15. Look for a yellow sign in the market's northwest corner.

A few major tourist attractions within a 15-minute walk of Mordi e Vai include the Mattatoio Modern Art Museum, the Rome War Cemetery and the Porta San Paolo. If traveling by Metro, the Piramide station on line B sits closest. Or take bus #75 or #83. Mordi e Vai is open Monday through Saturday from 8AM to 3PM.

## Links

WEBSITE: mordievai.it

GOOGLE MAP: goo.gl/maps/jjSTWybkTf92

# 47

# Panini and... Tapas?

Yes, the Spanish invented tapas. But why should they have all the fun? People the world over enjoy small dishes. The Romans, too! For a spot of Spain in the Eternal City, check out an exceptional, rustic Rome restaurant that's been a local favorite since 2004: PanDivino.

Created by an Italian husband and his Spanish wife, this casual restaurant serves a mix of traditional Italian and Spanish food. Although it's in the touristy Centro Storico, PanDivino is easy to miss if you're not looking for it. Once you find it, however, your reward is a superb selection of handmade Spanish and Italian dishes. Consider assembling a picnic by ordering your food to-go.

## Divine Dishes

The unique Spanish influence makes PanDivino's menu stand out. Tapas, paellas and Iberian wines are some Spanish favorites found here. For a filling meal, consider ordering the *tortilla de patatas*, a few empanadas or *paella de marisco*. The homemade charcuterie boards also hit the spot. Be sure to pair your Spanish fare with a refreshing glass of Salamancan wine.

On the Italian side, you'll notice that PanDivino has a special affinity for the Abruzzo region. This area, directly east of Rome, produces many of the wines offered here. And most of the sauces and chutneys draw inspiration from traditional Abruzzo recipes. There are many superb "grab-and-go" picnic options at PanDivino, including panini, wraps and salami. Oh, and don't worry if you're not a carnivore, you'll find veggie-friendly plates, too.

Before you leave, pick up a roll of fresh-baked Spanish bread or Italian focaccia. You should also indulge in a slice of traditional tiramisu or chocolate almond cake. Come on, go for it. You can skip the dessert when you get back home.

## How to Find It

PanDivino is right in the action. Travelers doing the grand tour of Rome should have no problem squeezing in a lunch or two here. Famous attractions within a 10-minute walk include the Pantheon, Campo de' Fiori, Largo di Torre Argentina, Piazza Navona and Museo di Roma.

The official address is Via del Paradiso, 39. The closest bus stops include C.so Vittorio Emanuele/Argentina and Rinascimento. It's not convenient to reach PanDivino via Metro.

PanDivino is open from 12:30PM to 7:30PM on Wednesday through Friday, 12:30PM to 8:30PM on Saturday, 12:30PM to 4:30PM on Sunday and 12:30PM to 3:30PM on Monday. The restaurant is closed on Tuesday.

## Links

WEBSITE:
facebook.com/PanDivino-Street-Food-559613234140028

GOOGLE MAP: goo.gl/maps/2cHUXmcuHTo

# 48

# A Cozy Hideout

**W**hen you're looking for a hearty meal in the heart of Rome, it's time to pay Old Bear a visit. No, we're not talking about a real bear! Old Bear is a unique restaurant in central Rome that offers guests all the comforts of a wooden cabin without having to worry about bone-chilling temps. Or bear attacks.

Named partly after the nearby Via dell'Orso ("*orso*" means "bear") and partly after its rustic ambiance, Old Bear has everything you'd expect from a wilderness lodge: wooden furniture, rustic lanterns, stone walls with exposed beams and a stuffed black bear at the front door. (Obviously.)

## Mouthwatering Morsels

Like any good Italian restaurant, Old Bear has a superb selection of pastas. However, the generous meat selection is where this restaurant shines. If you're a meat-and-potatoes person, then Old Bear is the place for you. One of the most popular menu items is a huge slab of grilled beefsteak with roasted potatoes.

Another hearty meat dish is the beef entrecôte with baked potatoes for two.

Old Bear also makes incredible pasta and seafood dishes. Try the *cacio e pepe*, *spaghetti alla carbonara* and sea bass carpaccio. One of their most famous pasta dishes is its innovative pumpkin lasagna. Yes, you read that right, pumpkin-flavored lasagna!

Be sure to bring a bear-sized appetite with you because you don't want to miss out on the homemade desserts. A few signature treats include boiled apples in red wine sauce, dark chocolate cake, Nutella mousse and cheesecake with fresh strawberries.

## How to Find It

Old Bear's official address is Via dei Gigli d'Oro, 2-4. It's within walking distance of many major attractions. The Pantheon is less than a 10-minute walk south. Other important tourist destinations within a 15-minute walk include Piazza Navona, Trevi Fountain and Spanish Steps.

For those using public transportation, the Senato bus stop is closest. You can reach Senato on bus N7 toward Clodio. Old Bear is open Monday through Saturday from 5PM to 12:30AM and closed on Sunday. It's highly recommended you book a table in advance, especially if you want to dine on Friday or Saturday. To reserve a table at Old Bear, call 06 682-100-09, email them at infooldbear@gmail.com or submit a contact form on the website.

## Links

WEBSITE: oldbear.it

GOOGLE MAP: goo.gl/maps/aeBjSWCQ61P2

# 49

# Classics with a Modern Twist

Despite a prime location in the eastern Monti neighborhood, Trattoria Morgana has yet to catch on with tourist hordes. Even though it's between between the Colosseum and Termini Station. This means you'll get an authentic meal for a reasonable price.

*breathes audible sigh of relief*

## What's Cooking?

Whether you're looking for an old standard or a fresh spin on an Italian classic, Trattoria Morgana will have something to suit your appetite. Unsurprisingly, the highlight is pasta. It's all made in-house and cooked to a superb al dente. A beloved classic is the fettuccine with meat sauce or porcini mushrooms. If you're craving something Asian-inspired, try the fettuccine with ginger cream. For a culinary adventure, why not try pasta tossed with oil and black cuttlefish ink?

Besides homemade pasta, they also have an extensive seafood selection. This includes *baccalà*, octopus, clams and grilled sea bream. And let's not forget their tantalizing meat options. With a focus on game like rabbit, they also grill steaks to perfection.

Definitely save room for dessert. Just a few delectable "*dolce*" options include tiramisu, *panna cotta* and cream caramel.

## How to Find It

The official address is Via Mecenate 19-21, a 5-minute walk from the Vittorio Emanuele Metro station. Keep your eyes peeled for a red-and-white awning above sidewalk tables and the "Trattoria Morgana" sign.

It's about 10 minutes walking from the Colosseum. From the Colosseo Metro stop, walk east on Via Nicola Salvi and turn towards Via della Domus Aurea. From here, take a left onto Via Mecenate. You will see Trattoria Morgana on your right-hand side.

Usually open for lunch and dinner with a break in-between, Trattoria Morgana serves lunch from 12:30PM to 3PM and dinner from 7PM to 11PM. Please note, they close every Wednesday. You can book a table at ahead of time by phone or visiting their website.

## Links

WEBSITE: trattoriamorgana.com

GOOGLE MAP: goo.gl/maps/7kccy9bTbzS2

# 50

## Hearty Pasta in the Heart of Rome

It's difficult to find an authentic meal at a reasonable price in Rome's touristy Centro Storico. However, even in the tourist-saturated Campo de' Fiori, you can find a good meal. Enter Osteria da Fortunata. This family run restaurant serves handmade pastas, decadent desserts and otherworldly oxtail.

Although restaurants abound in the Campo de' Fiori, you can easily spot Osteria da Fortunata. You can't miss the two women rolling out fresh pasta dough in the front window. Yes, these *mammas* literally roll out the pasta you will soon devour right before your eyes. You can't get more homemade than that. Unless you have an Italian *mamma* or *nonna*. If so, lucky you. Also, can I come over for dinner?

Open daily at noon, the food is so good here that you'll even find locals lined up for a table. Even if you must wait, it's well worth your time and easily the best value in this area of Rome.

## What's Mamma Cooking?

Osteria da Fortunata specializes in Roman comfort food, specifically pasta. The oxtail beef gnocchi, served under a mouthwatering mountain of parmesan, is a fan favorite. And by "fan" favorite, I mean "my" favorite.

They also make a fine *cacio e pepe* (pecorino and black pepper sauce). Other classic dishes include *strozzapreti* carbonara (elongated shell-like pasta), *sciavatelli amatriciana* (long, flatish noodles), *polpette umido* (meatballs in tomato sauce) and your choice of pasta mixed with artichokes and crispy pancetta. Top it all off with fresh *panna cotta* or a slice of tiramisu for dessert.

Please note, however, most of the employees don't speak perfect English. This is a good sign because it shows they don't cater only to foreign tourists. (Unlike many restaurants around it...) Brush up on your elementary Italian. And keep your Italian Food Decoder and Google Translate apps handy.

## How to Find It

The official address is Via del Pellegrino, 11/12. It's literally one minute from the center of Campo de' Fiori just beyond the fountain in the piazza's northwest corner. If you're using public transport, get on Metro Line B at Termini towards Laurentina and take this line until Circo Massimo. Once at Circo Massimo, hop aboard tram 8 towards Venezia and exit at Arenula/Cairoli.

## Links

WEBSITE: facebook.com/dafortunataallacancelleria

GOOGLE MAP: goo.gl/maps/5HacV55uNKr

# 51

# A Roman Gastropub

Quaff your thirst at one of Rome's most-historic pubs, L'Antica Birreria Peroni ("Ancient Peroni Brewery"). Cold beer and hearty food awaits just a stone's throw from many major attractions.

Now, even though it's neither ancient nor a brewery, this place rocks. Built in a former firehouse, this centrally located "gastropub" has been going strong since 1906. Fashioned in wood-and-timber Bavarian beer-hall style, L'Antica Birreria Peroni blends German and Italian influences into one of Rome's more unique dining establishments.

## What's on Tap?

L'Antica Birreria Peroni specializes in pouring, you guessed it, Peroni beer. Peroni, along with Moretti, is one of Italy's dominant beer brands. Although originally from Vigevano, they've produced Peroni in Rome since the 1860s. On tap, choose from the standard lager "Peroni Nastro Azzurro." Or step up to the award-winning, double-malt ale "Peroni Gran

Reserva" and the 100% Italian malt "Peroni Gran Riserva Rossa." They also pour a Fuller's London Pride for all you Anglophiles pining for the corner pub.

In keeping with the Bavarian theme, you'll notice German food on the menu. The most famous item is the "kilometer sausage"... which is exactly what it sounds like. Also, try their their take on German goulash. For local fare, consider the pasta carbonara, Roman tripe or pork beans (*fagioli all'uccelletto*).

By the way, for those who just can't get enough of all things Peroni, there is a Peroni Beer Museum ("Archivio Storico e Museo Birra Peroni") in Rome on Via Renato Birolli, 8. Call in advance to book a free weekday tour.

## How to Find It

Ideal for hungry sightseers, L'Antica is only about a five-minute walk south of the Trevi Fountain. From the Trevi Fountain, head west on Via delle Muratte, turn left at Via delle Vergini, turn right on Via dell'Umiltà and left on Via di S. Marcello. The Spanish Steps, Altare della Patria and the Giardini del Quirinale are all about 10 minutes away. For metro riders, the Barberini station is 10 minutes away.

Open Monday through Saturday from 12PM to 12AM, L'Antica Birreria Peroni doesn't accept reservations. Expect crazy crowds on Thursday, Friday and Saturday nights. So plan on arriving early, late or waiting at the boisterous bar for a table.

## Links

WEBSITES:

- Restaurant: anticabirreriaperoni.net
- Museum: birraperoni.it/museo

GOOGLE MAP: goo.gl/maps/nBE7u8T4RrB2

# 52

# The Pasta Workshop

I n recent years, Trastevere has become Rome's hotspot for foodies. The restaurants here are so popular it's growing difficult to find a decent-value meal. Or even an open table. There are, however, a few exceptional restaurants left. These place aren't yet overrun by tour groups and Instagrammers. One such eatery is Mr. Clood. This family run restaurant specializes in fresh, seasonal pasta dishes and features a continuously rotating menu.

## Plying the Pasta Trade

Mr. Clood brands itself as a *"laboratorio di pasta fresca"* ("fresh pasta workshop"). So, you'd better believe its reputation rests upon out-of-this-world handmade pastas. Its popular pasta dishes include gnocchi in tomato sauce, *straccetti* with radishes over pasta and pasta with shrimp, zucchini and tomatoes.

Mr. Clood also prides itself on serving a great variety of fresh seafood. A few fabulous fishy finds here include spaghetti with clams, salmon on a bed of arugula and sea bass with roasted potatoes. And my mouth is now watering.

As mentioned above, the menu changes with the seasons. So, always check the restaurant's chalkboard menu before committing.

## How to Find It

The official address of Mr. Clood is Via Luciano Manara, 13, which is close to the Palazzo di San Callisto. Other tourist attractions within a 15-minute walking distance of Mr. Clood include the Basilica of Our Lady in Trastevere and the Villa Sciarra Park. Bus #75 stops nearby at Morosini E. / Nuovo Regina Margherita.

Although well off the beaten tourist track, there's limited seating here. Therefore, make a reservation at least a day in advance. Book on their Facebook page or by calling +39 06 581 5186. Mr. Clood is open daily from 8AM to 3:30PM and 7PM to 10PM.

## Links

WEBSITE: facebook.com/Mr-Clood-1389522261291915

GOOGLE MAP: goo.gl/maps/Gc7Z8wkjpRP2

# 53

## Eating One Gelato a Day...

In Rome, you don't find the gelato... The gelato finds you! No matter where you turn in the Eternal City, you're bound to run into gelato shops ("*gelaterie*") serving up this cold-and-creamy treat. Every Roman has his/her opinion on which *gelateria* is the BEST IN ROME. But there's one walk-up gelato counter that receives high marks from locals and tourists: Frigidarium.

In central Rome, this family run gelato counter has been around for over 15 years. Frigidarium prides itself on making 100% natural gelato. It's as lovely to look at as it is delicious to devour. They never use artificial flavors or syrups. Plus, Frigidarium keeps prices reasonable. In fact, three scoops will only set you back about €3.

### The Fantastic Flavors of Frigidarium

The two main types of gelato are cream and fruit. Using only top-quality Sicilian pistachios, Frigidarium's pistachio remains its best seller. Some other favorites include chocolate, mint chocolate, *cremino* and Malaga (akin to rum and raisin).

Frigidarium tries hard to accommodate allergies. You will find egg-free, gluten-free and milk-free gelato. Don't expect sugar-free options... You are in a *gelateria*, after all.

Oh, and one more thing: Ask the gelato scoopers to put either a white or dark chocolate topping on your gelato. And ask for some whipped cream. You'll be glad you did.

Pro tip: After eating all those calories, consider running up the nearby Spanish Steps a few dozen times. Your waistline will thank you.

## How to Find It

Frigidarium's official address is Via del Governo Vecchio 112, which is just off the Piazza Navona. Tourist attractions within a 10-minute walk include the Pantheon, Chiesa di Santa Maria della Pace, Campo de' Fiori and Sant'Agnese in Agone. The closest bus stop is on the N15 line at C.so Vittorio Emanuele/Navona, a two-minute walk away.

Open daily, Frigidarium throws open the counter window from 10:30AM to 2AM, closing at 1:30AM on Sundays.

## Links

WEBSITE: frigidarium-gelateria.com

GOOGLE MAP: goo.gl/maps/4Qsqn7oeZuA2

# Leave a Review

Did you enjoy this book?

Feel it was a strong value? Are you interested in leaving feedback so that I may improve future editions?

If so, please leave a review on Amazon.

Leaving a review lets Amazon know that people are engaged and interested in this book and will help generate more exposure for it. There are millions of books on Kindle, so your review means a lot to help lift this modest title above the fray.

Thank you!

# FREE Travel Planning Email Courses

These 100% free email courses break down daily itineraries into digestible and customizable travel plans. Sent every morning on consecutive days, my travel-planning email courses will help you put together a trip that maximizes your time and budget, while minimizing itinerary potholes. Sign up today and your course begins tomorrow.

## 10 Perfect Days in Paris

Over five daily emails, we'll map out exactly where to go, how to get there and even provide suggestions for restaurants and picnic locations along the way. With over 5,000 graduates, this is our most-popular email course to date.

**Sign up:** bit.ly/perfectpariscourse

## 3 Blissful Days in Amsterdam

Three high-intensity sightseeing days scour Amsterdam's biggest sights, coolest neighborhoods, tastiest foodie haunts and feistiest night spots. You'll receive three daily emails breaking down exactly what to see and do and where to shop, eat and drink.

**Sign up:** bit.ly/3daysamsterdam

# FREE Paris eBook

Receive a FREE Paris ebook today.

After downloading your free book, you'll receive a monthly VIP email with book giveaways, new book announcements and huge book discounts ONLY available exclusively to subscribers.

Join the crew and subscribe for **FREE** to Rory Moulton's monthly email newsletter about European travel, "*EuroExperto*." In addition to the giveaways and discounts, receive the month's best European travel articles, news, tips, trends and more. I'll never spam you. I don't do ads. And you can unsubscribe at any time.

Smarter European travel is just a click away:
rorymoulton.com/subscribe

# Also by Rory Moulton

## Essential Paris Travel Tips

*"A very worthwhile tool when planning a Paris visit. Author presents idea after idea and ways to save anyone time and money... Worth every penny for this easy to use guide."*
5/5 stars, Amazon Best Seller
**Buy Now:** amzn.to/2yVdKV1

## Essential Amsterdam Travel Tips

*"Highly recommended with plenty of useful information. Light reading unlike other travel books – website links embedded are very helpful. Well worth the price."*
5/5 Stars, Amazon Best Seller
**Buy Now:** amzn.to/2Qjp3Nn

## Hiking France

Hike through pastoral countryside, stopping in beautiful villages, tasting wine at storied vineyards, sleeping in historic hotels, shopping country markets, stumbling upon Roman ruins and eating in some of Europe's best restaurants. **Coming in 2021!**

# About the Author

My name's Rory Moulton. I'm a writer, editor, book author and entrepreneur living in the Colorado Rockies with my wife and son. When away from my desk, I'm passionate about travel, woodworking, museums and the great outdoors. And beer. I also really like beer.

When it comes to travel—my passion of passions, and likely the reason you're here—I adamantly advocate for independent, ground-level budget travel. Here are my tenets for satisfying travel:

Focus on experiential—not checklist— travel. Go. See. Do. Make memories. Above all, stay in the moment. Furthermore, Instagram accounts aren't required.

Eat and shop local. Don't seek the tastes and comforts of home. After all, experiencing the strange and new is exactly why we leave home.

Stay in family run hotels and guesthouses, small hostels or neighborhood Airbnbs.

Meet local families. Practice their language.

Picnic in parks, church steps, alpine meadows, cliffside

beaches.

Ride overnight trains. Book passage by ferry. Take public transportation.

Sit in the cheap seats.

Eat street food.

See the major cultural sights *before* or *after* the crowds. Even if it means getting a little creative.

Avoid glossy tourist traps in all iterations. Be they plastic restaurants, overwrought (and overpriced) attractions or entire destinations.

Plan ahead. However, prepare to chuck the itinerary on a moment's notice when spontaneity calls.

Slow down.

In sum, ditch the all-inclusive, find an affordable flight to a foreign country, fill a carry-on backpack and off you go!

**You can connect with me on:**

🌐 https://rorymoulton.com

🐦 https://twitter.com/roryam

📘 https://www.facebook.com/EuroExperto

📎 https://www.instagram.com/rorymoulton

**Subscribe to my newsletter:**

✉ https://www.rorymoulton.com/subscribe